STRUCTURES OF IMAGE COLLECTIONS

FROM CHAUVET-PONT-D'ARC TO FLICKR

HOWARD F. GREISDORF

AND

BRIAN C. O'CONNOR

LIBRARIES UNLIMITED

A Member of the Greenwood Publishing Group

Westport, Connecticut • London

Library of Congress Cataloging-in-Publication Data

Greisdorf, Howard F.
   Structures of image collections : from Chauvet-Pont-d'Arc to Flickr / Howard
F. Greisdorf and Brian C. O'Connor.
       p. cm.
   Includes bibliographical references and index.
   ISBN-13: 978-1-59158-375-2 (alk. paper)
   1. Photographs—Conservation and restoration. 2. Photograph collections—
Conservation and restoration. 3. Image processing—Digital techniques.
4. Digital preservation. 5. Information storage and retrieval systems—Photographs.
I. O'Connor, Brian Clark. II. Title.
   TR465.G752 2008
   771—dc22   2007033044

British Library Cataloguing in Publication Data is available.

Library of Congress Catalog Card Number: 2007033044
ISBN: 978-1-59158-375-2

First published in 2008

Libraries Unlimited, 88 Post Road West, Westport, CT 06881
A Member of the Greenwood Publishing Group, Inc.
www.lu.com

Printed in the United States of America

The paper used in this book complies with the
Permanent Paper Standard issued by the National
Information Standards Organization (Z39.48–1984).

10   9   8   7   6   5   4   3   2   1

This publication is dedicated to my grandchildren, Sarah, Aaron, Kate, and Sami. The next generation of image collectors.

Howard Greisdorf

To my parents, Don and Marge, and their Argus C3.

Brian C. O'Connor

CONTENTS

PREFACE

AS WITH SO many printed works in the early twenty-first century, some aspects of this book are likely to seem passé or quaint by the time it is printed. We have endeavored to stay away from particular products and services, though of course some are prominent in certain discussions. We do not mean to endorse a particular product, service, or routine; rather, we use some simply as examples.

We must also comment on another aspect of publication in the early twenty-first century, namely, the physical and conceptual gaps between a printed page and engagement with the Internet. It remains prohibitively expensive to print large numbers of full-size color images in an academic book. Even if the color images were available, the printed page does not enable the same level of interactive engagement of more recent media. We hope that you will use the grayscale images on the printed pages as stepping stones; and we likewise hope you visit the Web site for a gallery of the images in color and as a place to engage with us in a discussion of images.

It is worth taking a moment to explain some aspects of the images in the following pages. Most were made by us. With one notable exception that we will address below, the images that we did not make were made by family and friends. Some aspects of this decision are fairly obvious: copyright issues are reduced, collection searching is reduced, and we are quite sure that the images present just what we need them to present. What may be less obvious is why the quality of the images varies. Many of the images were shot with professional equipment at very high resolution and high production values, while others were made with consumer cameras under less than ideal conditions. We sought to use images to which most users could relate, for example, images of family events and settings, vacations, and hobbies. Please note that the images are so fundamental to our discussions that they have not been set off from the text with labels calling them "figure" or "illustration" as one would ordinarily expect in such a work.

The images of cave paintings on the cover and within the text are a special case. They were made in the cave at Chauvet-Pont-d'Arc in Vallon-Pont-d'Arc (Ardèche), France. They were provided to us by the French Ministry of Culture and Communication's Regional Direction for Cultural Affairs—Rhône-Alps, from their Regional Department of Archaeology. We are both delighted and most humbly thankful to be permitted the use of these images to enrich our discussions. We also wish to thank our colleague, Cecile Satin, for negotiating the acquisition of the images and rights.

We bring to this particular examination of image collections many years of image production and consulting experience, together with several years of academic research on the ways that people make and find and label and use photographs. While we have conducted research and published together, we do not always agree completely on every concept or the way it ought to be presented. In the following pages you will note occasional differences in style or terminology as one or the other of us takes the lead on a particular portion of the discussion. We hope that you will find this engaging and that you will consider joining in on the discussion.

Writing in the *Atlantic Monthly* in June 1859, Oliver Wendell Holmes wrote of photographs: "It has become such an everyday matter with us, that we forget its miraculous nature, as we forget that of the sun itself, to which we owe the creations of our new art." This was not even twenty years after the invention of the daguerreotype. Today picture making is almost a routine part of life, since one need no longer engage in darkroom work or even take film in for one-hour processing. Yet in the realm of human history, the making of photographs is just now upon us, with little history or study. Holmes wrote in the same 1859 article with passionate delight about the invention of photography:

> Under the action of light, then, a body makes its superficial aspect potentially present at a distance, becoming appreciable as a shadow or as a picture. But remove the cause,—the body itself,— and the effect is removed. The man beholdeth himself in the glass and goeth his way, and straightway both the mirror and the mirrored forget what manner of man he was. These visible films or membranous *exuviae* of objects, which the old philosophers talked about, have no real existence, separable from their illuminated source, and perish instantly when it is withdrawn.
>
> If a man had handed a metallic speculum to Democritus of Abdera, and told him to look at his face in it while his heart was beating thirty or forty times, promising that one of the films his face was shedding should stick there, so that neither he, nor it, nor anybody should forget what manner of man he was, the Laughing Philosopher would probably have vindicated his claim to his title by an explosion that would have astonished the speaker.
>
> This is just what the Daguerreotype has done. It has fixed the most fleeting of our illusions, that which the apostle and the philosopher and the poet have alike used as the type of instability and unreality. The photograph has completed the triumph, by making

a sheet of paper reflect images like a mirror and hold them as a picture.

This triumph of human ingenuity is the most audacious, remote, improbable, incredible,—the one that would seem least likely to be regained, if all traces of it were lost,—of all the discoveries man has made.

We could in no way pretend to write in the manner of Holmes, but we do share his enthusiasm for photography and its role in the lives of individuals and cultures. It is likely that in any work that attempts to weave together elements from several disciplines and across 32,000 years of engagement with images, some readers will find that we have run roughshod over some concepts or highlighted some at the expense of others that might be equally useful. For any such errors of commission, omission, or inappropriate combination we take full blame. We only hope that the work as a whole will provoke thinking and picture making in ways that advance the discourse in this arena.

Acknowledgments

WE EXTEND our gratitude to all those whose conversations and critiques provided inspiration and guidance. Dr. Sue Easun at Libraries Unlimited gave equal measure of encouragement and prodding as our acquisitions editor. Without her efforts we would still have just lots of piles of notes for good ideas. Laura Smith guided the production process with a knowing hand.

Carole Greisdorf gave her loving support and encouragement throughout this arduous authoring journey. Lisa Rome provided insights into how she conducts digital image asset management in her professional life. Karen Greisdorf explained how she manages her images as a professional photographer. Painter and magazine publisher Jean Newman was kind enough to share her professional insights.

Mary O'Connor shared her thoughts and critiques as an art reproduction photographer and as a spouse tolerant of the writing process. Ethan and Andrew O'Connor provided technical critiques from engineering and artistic viewpoints.

While any book is the product of the thoughts, efforts, and tolerance of many folks, we take all blame for running rough-shod over concepts and insights of others and for any missteps and misunderstandings.

PART I

SEEING AND BELIEVING

Imagine a group of people a long time ago, say, 30,000 years. They lived their lives, they had dreams, they cared for their children, they had ideas about their place in the world. How would they share all this with their children? How would they remember and pass on their experiences and their thoughts? How would they let others know they had "been here"? One way they did these things links them directly to us—they made pictures, sometimes collections of pictures.

A lovely linguistic connection highlights the interconnection of image collections across generations. Several of the animal figures in the collection in the Chauvet-Pont-d'Arc cave were drawn with a finger moving on a thin film of clay. In French the term for such drawing is *tracé digital*, or digital drawing. We are at once

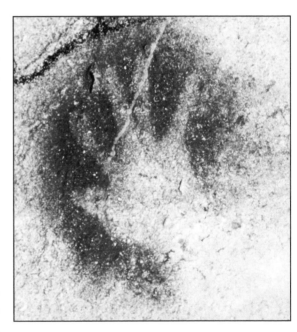

Panel of the Hand Stencil, Grotte Chauvet-Pont-d'Arc, slide no. 4.

linked from twenty-first-century digital images to the digital images of our ancestors, reminded that the computer-based use of the term is anchored in our very physical nature and reminded that construction of images is a purposeful act.

Panel of the Horses. Adapted from Grotte Chauvet-Pont-d'Arc, slide no. 12.

What does this group of horse images mean? On one level our only answer must be: "We do not know." We are not sure whether these are icons of some shamanistic ritual, or talismans for hunting parties, or simply images that amused their makers. We do not even know who the makers were. What we do know is that the images in the Chauvet caves in France date back over 30,000 years and they form a collection of pictures.

In the twenty-first century, a group of horse images is likely to look something like this set derived from the flickr.com Web site. We may know

the name of the photographer; we may even have a few descriptive terms; we may think that these images look "more realistic"; yet, on the face of it, we know nearly as little about our twenty-first-century horses as those pictured at Chauvet. What we do know is that we have a span of over 30,000 years of image collecting by humans.

VENI, VIDI, VICI

In 47 BCE Julius Caesar accomplished a major military victory. In advance of his return to Rome he sent the Roman Senate his famous message, usually translated as "I came, I saw, I conquered." If we look a little more closely at the Latin words, we might do Caesar a bit more justice, and at the same time come up with a motto for *Homo sapiens*. If we look to the etymologies and uses of the words sent by Caesar to the Senate, we might restate the translation as something rather more rich, perhaps: "I arrived on the scene, I understood the situation, I was successful."

> věnǐo, **věni**, ventum: *To come* [I came]
>
> vǐděo, **vǐdi**, vǐsum: *To see, perceive, to see* with the mind's eye, *mark, observe, discern, understand, comprehend, be aware, know* [I saw, I comprehended]
>
> vincō **vīcī**, vīctus: In war, *to conquer, overcome, get the better of, defeat, subdue, vanquish, be victorious: To prevail, succeed, overcome, win* [I conquered, I succeeded]
>
> Charlton T. Lewis, Charles Short, *A Latin Dictionary* Perseus Project at www.perseus.tufts.edu

Of course, translation is a tricky business, but our point here is that even the Romans of 2,000 years ago understood, as do we, that "I see" may well mean more than "I have visible wavelength energy stimulating electrical activity in my eyeballs and brain." Seeing enables understanding and resolution of problems, or in the words of Fischler and Firschein:

> When a person says "I see" after solving a difficult mathematical or conceptual problem, he is voicing a piece of wisdom that we are just beginning to appreciate, that his perceptual machinery... probably played a substantial role in producing the solution.

Debate over the human journey continues; but we do know that for several million years hominid brains developed more complex visual capabilities, sacrificing some attributes of more "primitive" species, while gaining unique attributes of distinction and integration. Fischler and Firschein comment: "Most of the human brain is involved in visual perception and...intelligence evolved to support the perceptual process."

BUT WE FORGET

Human vision is complex and integral to human thinking. But we forget images. We are not perfectly capable of remembering each surface, line, and color of our child's face as it was twenty years ago. We are not perfectly capable of using words and gestures to transfer a complex visual image into the mind of another. We are not perfectly capable of comparing large numbers of images in our minds to look for small anomalies or compare large numbers of image details. Our eye-brain systems are well suited to enabling us to thrive in our environments, but not so fully capable of supporting newer cultural needs and uses of images.

Similar to forgetting is the inability to put our eyes everywhere there might be something to see. We might want to see Niagara Falls, an armadillo, what our child looked like when he broke his wrist years ago, the site of the start of the Free Speech Movement, or an old New England library decorated for the holidays.

SO WE COLLECT

Human collection of images is an ancient practice. We use images and text to trace how visual objects have worked their way into our lives as experiential artifacts of various colors, shapes, textures, and proportions that, for reasons bearing

> For our purposes we define the concepts of *collect* (verb) and *collection* (noun) as follows:
>
> *Collect: To gather together into one place or group; to gather, get together.*
>
> *Collection: A number of objects collected or gathered together, viewed as a whole; a group of things collected and arranged.*
>
> Oxford English Dictionary

philosophical and psychosocial scrutiny, have led to collections of myriad description. Why we collect, how we collect, how we use these collections, and how we build, maintain, and access collections of images are the focal points of this book. We hope to push the boundaries of understanding the concept of "collection." We hope to guide, provoke, intrigue, and engage anyone who thinks about what they see, anyone who uses images to think and to do things.

Perhaps one could use the Library of Congress subject headings in a card catalog to search for individual images; or search through titles arranged alphabetically for DVDs (a special form of image collection) in the local recycled bookstore. The card catalog could be used to represent all forms of media with multiple entry points, but it requires considerable expenditure of resources to create and maintain. Simple bins with alphabetical arrangement are simple and effective but with fewer possible configurations for access.

Do the objects within a collection necessarily have to be within some spatial boundary? Photographs of seagulls in Oakland, California, and Hampton Beach, New Hampshire, suggest that the answer is no.

Seagulls. Oakland, California; Hampton Beach, New Hampshire.

Do entities within some boundary necessarily constitute a collection?

Probably. One could always say the collection constitutes "those things that are in this place." If we take a step from that super set, it may be possible to say "no." Here is a picture of a bag of balloons that happened to fall next to a saddle at an Old West reenactment. There was no intentionality behind the sharing of space. The other image presents items in an office, some of which are the ordinary stuff of research and daily office conduct and other pieces of which happened to arrive with visitors and had no application or necessity.

Need anyone be able to see or use the entities within a collection?

The images in the Chauvet caves were available to the viewer only with difficulty, yet we could scarcely say they did not exist as an image collection. Digital files on a CD from the photo processor require a computer for viewing; otherwise, the CD is just a colorful coaster. In the early twentieth century, glass lantern slides were shipped about the country in wooden cases with screwed-down lids—dozens of images existed in a form viewable by the unaided eye, but unseeable by any but the rightful recipients.

Can one imagine a collection of entities that have never been within some set of spatial or temporal boundaries?

Yes, as with the gulls, we can easily imagine grouping like items, even if they were in existence at significantly different times and places. Here, mundane staples in a utility pole in Berkeley, California, sit well with staples imaged four years later on a utility pole in Denton, Texas.

Can there be a set of entities within close proximity and structured by some organizing principle that is not a collection?

A trash receptacle provides an intriguing counterexample to the balloons-and-saddle photograph. In a trash receptacle we have a case of the container itself defining a super set. While the individual entities may have no relationship to one another, they all have the quality or attribute of not being wanted. This

may, indeed, be a negative attribute, but it is one of significant validity in daily life.

Could one woman's collection be another man's meaningless chaos?

For some purposes the opportunity to see what is at hand may be more important than "neatness." While organizing concepts do tend to reduce expenditure of resources for searches conducted within some organizing concept, that

concept may stand in the way of use. So, is a messy desk a collection? It may well be a collection of items known to be useful, possibly useful, possibly catalytic, potentially related to something already in the pile, possibly related to something that will later be in the pile, possibly evocative of something formerly but not now in the pile, or hinting at an emptiness in the pile now at hand. Use and potential use being the operative concepts in place of a priori regulations.

Since nearly all entities are made of smaller parts, is almost everything a collection?

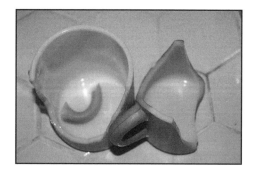

Are there any entities at all, or do we simply collect attributes (what things look like, taste like, feel like, sound like)? Do we just gather together, actually or figuratively, bits of the environment that suit some purpose?

Do multiple copies of one entity constitute a collection?

Some might argue that multiple copies of an entity simply present the same thing over and over. Yet, if we turn to purpose as an attribute of a collection, we can see that mere repetition may have its uses. One toy eagle could be given to a grandchild, a few could be used to hold down a picnic blanket, and several could be used as decoration in an office at the

 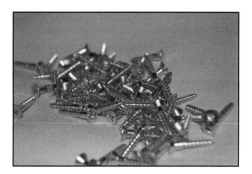

university for which this is the mascot. One screw can hold one end of the edge strip on a decked canoe, two can be used to hold both ends, and a screw every eight inches in between will provide a protective and decorative element for the boat.

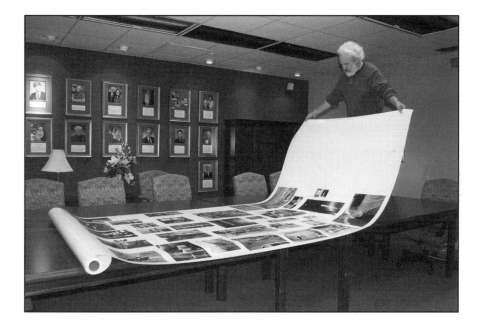

Image collections can be constructed in myriad ways, both physically and conceptually. Two dozen images of varying sizes and content may be printed on a single sheet of paper, while separate images of donors all printed to the same size and framed in the same manner may decorate the wall. Images may exist only digitally and require some mechanism for viewing; some may be public and others may be casual and private. Some may be formed intentionally and with considerable expenditure of resources, while others may be formed ad hoc, or even discovered inadvertently.

A Provocation on Image Access within a Collection

Given the popularity of Leonardo da Vinci's *Mona Lisa*, it is perhaps no surprise that a Google image search yields (at this writing) a collection of over 59,000 images. Some are reproductions of the whole painting, some are reproductions of just portions of the painting, some are manipulations, some are photos of pets named Mona Lisa, and some appear to be fashion or advertising photographs of women, with the term Mona Lisa simply adding an artistic cachet. This is probably no surprise. Recall, though, that we are looking at the special case of a collection of images that are all of one object. Recall that even if we exclude the images of pets and fashion models, we are still looking at a large collection of different images of the same object.

Three things are especially surprising about this large collection of Mona Lisa images. First, there is so much variety in the color characteristics, such as hue and luminance, that one must wonder which is closest to the original painting. Second, there is a large number of different croppings, especially the distance from top of head to upper image boundary. Third, in trying to answer the question of closeness to the original, one notices that the official photograph made by the staff of the Louvre is not to be found in the first ten pages of results. This means that most searchers will not likely find it. They will reach the futility point before they find the image by this means.

Even if one happens to know that Mona Lisa is sometimes spelled Monna Lisa, and one ignores the polite question from Google: "Did you mean to search for Mona Lisa?" the Louvre image as presented on the Louvre Web site does not show up in the image search. Now, it may be the case that some of the Mona Lisa images found at other Web sites are simply duplicated from the official Louvre image, but one would have to examine each document to find that out. Even if some are, indeed, derived from the Louvre image, one would want to know the extent of manipulation or the remove from the original image. Perhaps the easiest example of this would be the reduction of the number of pixels in the derived image as compared with the original image.

Then there is the corollary issue of the quality of the representation of the original Louvre photograph of the painting. While it might seem to be a fairly mechanical process, art reproduction actually is fraught with difficult decisions about the process of reproducing a three-dimensional object—the brush strokes reflect light in three dimensions—within a two-dimensional medium. Lighting poses other problems, such as evenness of illumination, specular highlights reflecting from glossy surfaces, shadows cast by the frame, and the myriad issues of color management.

THOUGHTS ON THE TEXT

We hope that these first few pages have raised enough questions and sparked enough interest for the reader that the concept of structuring image collections is no longer a mundane issue but the basis for challenging philosophical debate. In an effort to stimulate such debate, we have constructed the book as a collection of five parts, to first, define the nature of images (Part I: Seeing and Believing); next, describe how images are structured and used (Part II: The Language of Image Structures); third, discuss the nature of image collecting and its structures (Part III: Image Collections); fourth, consider how history and culture have molded our approaches to image collection (Part IV: Groupthink, Deindividuation, and Desensitivity); and finally, explore what the future portends for structuring more efficient and effective image collections (Part V: Lessons from the Future).

We have structured each chapter with a trifurcated approach for describing and explaining how mankind has traditionally engaged with visual objects, both real and perceived, as defined by the nature of the visual objects themselves, their historical underpinnings, and the psychosocial aspects that relate visual experience with human cognition for structuring collections of images. We make no claim to advancing the research front in the areas of the paleosciences, ethnography, philosophy, human physiology, perception, cognition, social psychology, art history, information science, collection development, cataloguing, or indexing, but we do bring to bear some small part of the fruitful work done in these various disciplines on how we might be able to structure images we collect more effectively.

Image (adapted from the *Oxford English Dictionary*)

L. *imago, imagin-em*: imitation, copy, likeness, statue, picture, phantom; conception, thought, idea; similitude, semblance, appearance, shadow.

1. An artificial imitation or representation of the external form of any object, esp. of a person, or of the bust of a person.
2. a. An optical appearance or counterpart of an object, such as is produced by rays of light either reflected as from a mirror, refracted as through a lens, or falling on a surface after passing through a small aperture.

CHAPTER ONE

DO WE NEED TO SEE?

If we are capable of knowing what is where in the world, our brains must somehow be capable of representing this information – in all its profusion of color and form, beauty, motion, and detail.

David Marr, *Vision*

EVIDENCE POINTS TO the affirmative by confirming an evolutionary sequence of adaptations to light intensities that spanned hundreds of millions of years leading from eye spot to eye cup to eye chamber. All of these developments emerged as an enhanced way for the seeing organism to cope more effectively with the environment into which it had been cast. While the ensuing discussion and succeeding chapters make no attempt to describe the physiological aspects of this developmental process over time, the discourse included is concerned with what seeing is all about, particularly from the human perspective.

Seeing is a process of collecting and storing images for use in meeting the psychosocial needs of an individual. Although other human sensory systems (hear, smell, touch, and taste) perform similar supporting roles, it appears that vision is the prime input for generating the greatest understanding of the outside world. Although the visually impaired can lead healthy productive lives in today's modern society, we suggest that quite the opposite was true when hominid evolution was in its infancy. There is no fossil evidence that suggests other than two eyes for seeing the surrounding environment for the purpose of survival. Without visual senses, our ancestors' survival was probably a short-lived experience. What we often forget, however, is that human visual development, as revealed in research findings, has most likely been an evolutionary process, beginning with raw vision and proceeding to our present-day understanding of the visual process as a fully integrated system of seeing, thinking, and speaking.

It would be fair to posit that how we organize and structure collections of images is as much a function of "how we see" as it is a function of "how we think." The nature of this symbiotic relationship produces a physiology that compels us to organize our visual engagements with the outside world. That organizational process begins with discrimination. Simply stated, the discriminating mind takes the input from the impartial eye and translates the neural information into a bifurcated universe of dichotomous entities that

identify an image based on categories of "what it is" and "what it is not." Over time, those categories have increased to the point that almost everything we see must have a name attached to it. We seldom see without naming, albeit the naming may often be a subconscious process. For example, in the images of potatoes and tomatoes here, we may not be sure it is a "potato" but know very well it is not a "tomato." Of course, here we have a sign that helps.

If we step back and view the world as our early predecessors likely did, we must start with how we capture the world around us through our eyes. Indeed, how we structure images as sensory input. Until recently, much was known about what we could see, but relatively little was known about how we see. With the latest research stemming from new technologies at our disposal, we now recognize that the path from object to eye to brain is an intricate, complex process that encompasses numerous aspects of seeing dating back to humankind's earliest efforts at survival. Without subjecting the reader to a treatise on eye/brain physiology, the short story is that vision appears to be an integrated parallel process that engages several layers of neural activity simultaneously. If we view that process sequentially, we first see lines, then curves, and then complex curves—in essence, we see edges—and as most of us discover soon after birth, objects are recognized first by the edges that form their shapes.

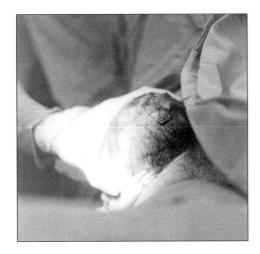

As we gain comfort from being able to identify objects by the edges that outline their shapes, the eye/brain process also detects differences in texture and luminosity that contribute to visual acuity, including how faded or washed out the image is in the human field of vision.

In addition to seeing edges, often the sharpness of those edges is not only a factor of our own visual acuity, but also of the difference between a perceived object and its background. Aspects of visual contrast can often obscure an observer's understanding of the object(s) being viewed. Thus, contrast becomes another factor that structures an image, and its interpretation, as provided in the examples below.

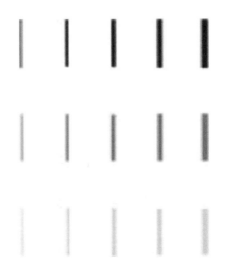

How many lines do you see? How sharp are they?

Very low, nominal, and very high contrast images of the same fruit.

PARTS, PIECES, AND PATTERNS

In a few paragraphs we have now defined the essence of seeing a structured image. Without consideration, yet, for color, depth, orientation, or motion, the ability to see shapes, see them with some clarity, and distinguish them from the shadows paves the way for higher-order visual processing. A next step is the ability to understand the meaning and nature of the objects we see by recognizing their edges and shapes as they form individual or more complex parts and pieces within the visual landscape. This processing is often referred to as *pattern recognition*. We know what we are seeing because we recognize familiar patterns in our visual field. Those patterns include not only objects themselves but also the spaces between them.

Observe the objects below. What differentiates one from another? What makes their image structures the same?

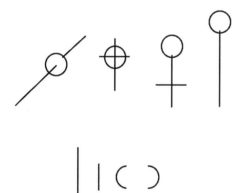

Edges, shapes, and patterns.

There's really not much to see, but my mind thinks there's more than meets the eye in the next picture of watermelons. Even with variations in contrast, many viewers will likely be able to derive "melonness" just from edge data in an image such as this, particularly if they have seen a similar image with a more "normal" amount of data.

Humans have always been able to see. Having the capability to scan the environment and see shapes clearly had a major impact on sustenance, survival, and perpetuation of the species. But everyone did not necessarily harbor the same sights. Before early hominids could speak about what they saw, they could only capture and process the visual stimuli that were products of their surroundings; and as brain capacity increased, the ability to remember what was seen became easier. Not all humans see all shapes and shadows with the same sharpness. And all humans that see with the same sharpness do not necessarily see the same shapes or the same shadows. In essence, we all see the same objects in different ways.

Early hominids most likely would have been able to see the same way that you see. However, in the early stages of cognitive development, they most probably were unable to describe what was being seen. Language, as we know it today, was likely missing. Hence, lines of similar length, thickness, and orientation most likely provided little value to the discriminatory abilities of our early ancestors. And, even if the images did have meaning, there was no way for that information to be effectively communicated to others. It would appear that lines, whether straight or curved, as viewed by these early predecessors were valued only for their ability to circumscribe shapes that could be distinguished one from another. Millions of years later, we are doing the same thing. What we see represents the edges to which we choose to direct our attention.

Image structure begins with lines and curves that establish shape, aided by associated characteristics and defined by shadows and a level of luminosity (contrast). To see is to see shapes. Humans need to see shapes and be able to differentiate one from another. Image structure is thus, first, a process of visual differentiation based on individual sensory capabilities.

One of the difficulties in presenting a coherent discussion on the nature and structures of image collections is the requirement to define *meaning* in the context of viewing, collecting, storing, and retrieving images for useful endeavors. Our particular view is a synthesis of several ideas that consider *image meaning* as a relationship between the raw elements of an image (lines, curves, shadows,

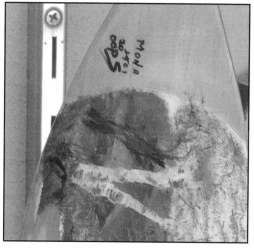

We often see only what we want to see and miss all the rest.

and contrasts) and human experience. Even the highly influential philosophy of Martin Heidegger (1889–1976) construed *meaning* as strictly a function of disclosure between those raw elements and the viewer. However, once we limit our understanding of an image to only a set of categories with which we are most familiar, we have a tendency to fail to notice other actual features.

Appearance

Although most of us have the ability to receive the same light, we each process that information in a different manner. Those individualized processes produce *appearances*. An appearance, in simplest terms, is a mental representation. In an expanded sense, however, appearance is a visual editorial that renders a visually reinforced opinion. Just as we think and speak our opinions in words, we also have the ability to see visual expressions of those same opinions.

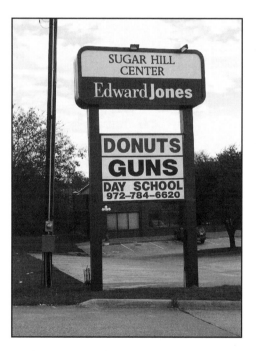

Is this just a shopping center sign or does it tell us something more?

We often see not what an observance *is*, but what an observance *appears to be*. As a result, we tend to live, work, and play in two different worlds, constantly vacillating between them. One being the world of perception, filled with appearances, and the other being the world of conception, filled with words based on how we think. This bifurcation of human visual activity is best described by author Stephen Hogbin, artist, designer, instructor, and lecturer, in his publication titled: *Appearance and Reality: A Visual Handbook for Artists, Designers and Makers.*

In the following discussion of image collection structure, we have taken Hogbin's framework and synthesized what we pose as an underlying problem in the struggle to associate words with images caused by this idea of perception/conception duality of human visual experience. As is often the case in trying to create structure around a collection of images, this duality can confound, disrupt, and even destroy the visual contiguity that is trying to be achieved.

In the following diagram, we offer an explanation of this duality by providing the reader with a visual perception along with an associated verbal conception.

PERCEPTION
What the eye sees and
the body experiences

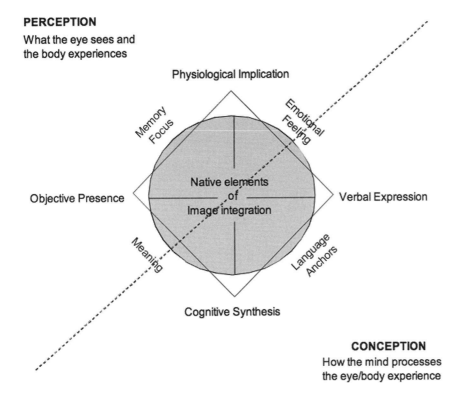

CONCEPTION
How the mind processes
the eye/body experience

Perception / Conception Duality

In the diagram, perception is composed of two key components: objective presence and physiological implication. *Objective presence* is what we see based on color, shape, texture, distance, contrast, luminance, and acuity. *Physiological implication* is the physical reaction invoked by the visual experience based on heart rate, skin response, and like sensory responses. The ancillary components of perception are derived from what is remembered (*memory focus*) about what is being seen, the meaning applied to those memories, and the emotional feelings that stem from the physiological implications. All of this can take place as a visual observance in the absence of conceptual attachments (words).

Similarly, conception is also composed of two key components: cognitive synthesis and verbal expression. *Cognitive synthesis* is the ability to mentally merge and meld the perceptual components into a communicative format as an expression of understanding, that is, "I know what I am seeing" or "I don't know what I am seeing." *Verbal expression* is simply the ability to communicate information about what is being seen. The ancillary components of conception are derived from the language of the observer (*language anchors*) in conjunction with the meaning and emotional feeling elicited from the visual perception in order to generate a verbal response.

Appearance, as a visual process, is composed of both perception and conception. On the one hand, appearance is equivalent to induction, whereby one proceeds from generalization to derive specific conclusions (opinions). On the other hand, appearance is equivalent to intuition, whereby one proceeds from specific conclusions (opinions) to derive visual generalizations. Hence, appearances are simply perceptual and conceptual deposits that function as the total visual experience of an individual observer.

The problem, or difficulty, associated with this human approach to visual experience is that seeing and saying may have meaning to one observer, but that same visual experience may or may not have the same meaning to another observer. From an image collection perspective, attention to how a collection is structured will influence the appearances derived from the perceptions and conceptions of individual observers.

As Alfred North Whitehead concluded, when we get lost in schemes of simplification, we tend to get lost in "fallacies of misplaced concreteness." Once man moved beyond seeing and developed into a thinking, speaking being, any image that acted as sensory input could be processed with multiple strands of meaning. And, in support of that view, we might turn to Nietzsche by repeating that value lies in our interpretations, and every elevation of man brings with it the overcoming of narrower interpretations. While the structure of an image may be concrete, the meaning of that image is open to a multitude of interpretations. S. I. Hayakawa may have said it best: "To see in limited modes of vision is not to see at all." This dilemma leaves us with a daunting task when it comes to structuring image collections.

CHAPTER TWO

Living with Vision

DO WE NEED TO SEE IN COLOR?

Perhaps not, but it helps. Visual evolution moved from structures that merely distinguished light (white) from dark (black) to a neurally functioning brain that had a new attribute: it could distinguish color. From a survival perspective, color was certainly an enhancement to the sensory arsenal that allowed our earliest ancestors to effectively cope with the existing environment. And color was assuredly a way to distinguish foodstuffs that were edible from those that were unfit for consumption.

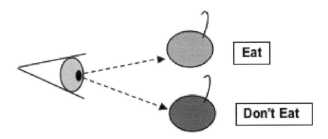

Color also allows for a finer-grained distinction among visual objects and goes beyond shape recognition to help define the condition of viewed objects.

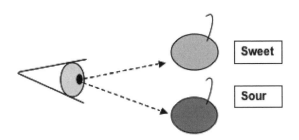

In addition to object identification and condition, color also fosters feelings of emotional impact that shape alone cannot do.

It should now be apparent that *image structure* is how meaning is communicated to the viewer. In addition to an object's shape, as defined by its edges, an object's color provides another layer of meaning in the mind of the beholder. Human adults with normal color vision can identify approximately 150 different

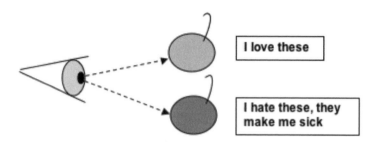

colors, and when aspects of color saturation and brilliance are introduced, discriminatory capabilities can increase into the millions. The visual significance of color in the context of image collection is that color can translate immediately into an emotional quality, as illustrated in the figure above. As Barry posits in her book *Visual Intelligence*, "so powerful is the psychological effect of color that it will sometimes override all other practical considerations."

All in all, color is cool (or hot, depending on your choice of metaphors) because it can complement image structures in so many ways. Similar to shape, color is a visual experience. In contrast to shape, which can also be sensed tactilely, color is strictly a visual sensation. You cannot differentiate colors by holding, touching, hearing, smelling, or tasting them. You can only experience color by seeing it.

At this juncture we could say that all images are structured from shape and color. We can also say that we have not yet mentioned the other supporting characteristics of image structure that make the experience of seeing so spectacular. However, without shape and without color there is no image. Even black and white (and shades of gray) are capable of adequately defining images. However, those readers who have had the experience of unexpectedly walking into a glass door will fully understand. Without color you can't see it. And, sometimes that hurts.

Humans are considered to be trichromatic (able to see combinations of red, blue, and green) when it comes to color vision, and the research literature abounds with discussions of cones, wavelengths, reflectance, hue, saturation, and luminance to render understanding of this concept. However, our immediate concern is that color values do influence the seeing eye and the thinking brain in ways that can affect the nature of image collections.

WHERE AM I?

Having discussed two of the central aspects of the visual experience (shape and color), we think it is important to note that an integrated whole in the human visual field is not complete until a perceptual synthesis takes place that includes the additional elements of orientation and depth. Image structure is not only a matter of color, shape, and texture; it is also about size, location, and perspective.

When considering size, the discussion isn't always about how big or small an object is, but how the object is viewed cognitively from a visual perspective in terms of its location and orientation as seen by the viewer. For example, how many white croquet balls are shown in the figure below?

The answer is one. You're just seeing the image structured from six different viewing distances. Referring back to the prior discussion about how we see, you also notice that you perceive a white croquet ball, not a white croquet circle. Why? You see the curves, you see the edges, and you see the shadows. Voila! It is a ball . . . and it's white.

Now let's take another look at our white croquet ball.

Why does it look like it's hanging from the ceiling? You don't play croquet on the ceiling. It must not be a white croquet ball. What happened to our image structure? Nothing. What changed was the perceived need to categorize the image as something else. If you're finding this concept somewhat perplexing, indeed it is. Look very closely at the image below and then describe it to yourself in one word.

The concept of orientation is very important when it comes to image structure. Without taking into account which edges are up and which are down, we often find it difficult to describe objects in the visual field. However, our ability to sense our own orientation to the outside world is not at issue here; all that we see is viewed from a variety of orientations, and often those orientations create confusion, especially when we are called upon to describe the objects or scene being viewed. Recall now how you described the image above; take a look at it now and describe it in one word.

What happened to the first image? Where is the square? It's still there, just tilt your head. But if you don't, you'll probably call this image a diamond. Why should we concern ourselves over such simple representations of image structure? The answer lies in the visual complexity generated from the combination of image structures, image collections, and the structures of image collections. For clarification, we have taken the two images and recast them below as a two-image collection with shading added.

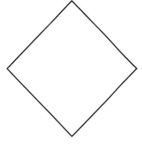

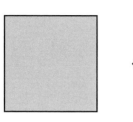

First, we have two visual representations with the same image structure, that is, gray four-sided figures. Second, we have an image collection consisting of two gray four-sided figures. Third, we have a structured collection that contains squares, squares and diamonds, gray objects, rhombic figures, parallelograms, polygons, figures with straight edges, and objects with angles. The task of defining images in a structured collection can be daunting, albeit a straightforward process of seeing shapes at varying distances and in different orientations. It is not the images that create havoc with structuring their collections; the words we choose to describe them generate problems.

Let us make a small probe beyond these simple geometric shapes with an image scanned from a college humor magazine from some time ago. The premise of the piece was "improbable trips," a reference to drug use on college campuses in the 1960s. The author sets about discovering "legal natural

Photo by Skean & O'Connor, 1968

"Improbable Trips," by Al Skean. *Dartmouth Jack-O-Lantern*, 60 (3), 1968.

phenomena guaranteed to take you away from reality." The photographs of the "away from reality" situations were simple images of the author in ordinary settings with slight twists on the lighting or composition and the help of captions. The image here uses not quite realistic combinations of simple shapes, inversion, and shadows to present the "Sleep Trip" on which the author reported: "This trip was the most peaceful of all, but coming down proved to be a pain."

Inverting the image presents us with something rather different. A figure asleep on the floor is "acceptable," while the upside-down chair and print are merely distracting. It is obviously not a man sleeping on the ceiling that causes us, as we move from seeing to a mode of describing, a sense of descriptive paralysis. Because the image plays with our senses overtly, we might easily apply an adjective such as "weird," or "strange," or even "impossible." However, it is often the case that image searchers may be looking for just such weird images to fit current needs.

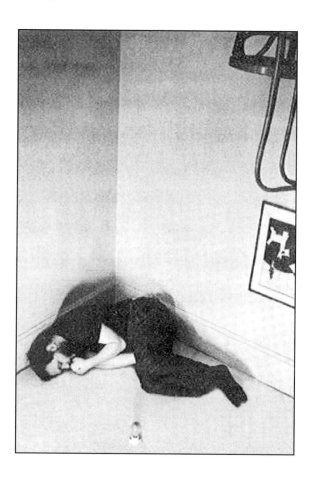

CHAPTER THREE

SEEING AND COLLECTING

Collections are implements meant to enhance and restore a person's sense of self.

Werner Muensterberger

WHY DO WE collect things? Because we can't resist! Most readers will likely assume that our emphasis is on structuring collections that include pictures of things. To the contrary, we will use pictures of things to emphasize how people tend to structure collections. The subtlety of this distinction can be better understood by referencing the following table of image collections that reside, not in large institutional confines or even smaller well-known venues, but among the daily routines that make collecting part of the human condition.

Things collected	Reasons for collecting	How collections are built	How displayed or stored	Systems of collection organization
Coins	Monetary value	Online purchase	On walls	By label
Coffee cups	Memories			
T-shirts	I like them	Manuals/publications	On refrigerators	By cataloguing system
Stamps				
CDs	Professional interest	Word of mouth		By date of acquisition
Police badges			In boxes	
Photographs		Gifts from others		By geographic location
Greeting cards	Casual interest		In albums	
"Garbage Pail Kids"	Fun	Build it yourself		By shape or size
trading cards				
			On maps	By topic
Barbies	Ownership	From friends		By alphabetic order
Magnets			In bookcases	By value
Musical scores	Prestige or to impress others	Shop purchases		By unique attribute
Pocket calendars			In cabinets	By theme
Books		Flea markets		By event
Rejection letters	Keep a record		In protected vaults	
	To belong to a group			
		Trade with others		By chronological order
		Find without looking	In frames	By color code
	Social needs			

Each of the examples in the table represents a collection structure, albeit at a rudimentary level of collection organization, as described by a small group of PhD students in relation to things that they collected, why they collected those things, how they built their collections, how they kept their collections, and how their collections were organized.

The examples in the table point to the fundamental issues surrounding possible structures for image collections. But before we get into more detailed descriptions of these various approaches to collection structure, let us further clarify that a person does not have to see in order to access, organize, and store a collection of objects. Collection structure can just as easily be created around the kinesthetic values surrounding how something feels, tastes, or smells as it can around simply visual contexts.

UBIQUITOUS HOUSEHOLD COLLECTIONS

As we begin this portion of our discussion on collection structures, we recognize that from an ethnographic point of view not everyone lives in a location or environment that provides the luxury of a single-family dwelling unit where one's possessions can be safely kept. However, we also recognize that most of the people that fall into that category will most likely not be reading this book.

Many of us often lose sight of the fact that our daily lives are filled with opportunities to structure collections of images and image objects in our own homes, apartments, and offices. Our personal possessions are normally not considered collections; however, if you look around your own residence you will probably notice that a variety of the items you own are grouped in collection fashion. Notice that we said "grouped," because many of us tend to group like items in a single place without necessarily organizing them. In either case, each grouping can be viewed as a collection—with or without structure. Collections are, in a sense, physical manifestations of categories. They make life simpler by reducing the number of places we have to look for something.

As individual collectors of visually experienced sights, we can point to a multitude of "around the house" collections that many people take for granted; nonetheless, they often incorporate structures similar to those used by large institutions for accessing, viewing, and storing the objects in their collections. We offer but a few examples in the following discussion.

CLOSET COLLECTIONS

In all of the following examples and the accompanying photos, we intend to make it perfectly clear that the concept of an organized collection does not imply a sense of neatness or cleanliness. Dust may accumulate and things may not appear tidy, yet the objects can still be considered a structured collection. We begin with household closets, which we recognize as unique to every homeowner in terms of size and the objects stored in them. However, the common nature of closets is that they normally act as collection points

for clothes, shoes, and other wearing apparel that is not folded and put elsewhere.

As will become apparent with our continuing discussion about collection structure, we see some immediate issues surrounding collection organization. In the photos above, we see some general organization related to the size of the objects, that is, jackets of the same length hanging together and shoeboxes of similar size stacked together. We also note that jackets are not arranged by color, and shoes are not arranged by brand name, even though such tags could be used to structure the closet collection shown.

CABINET COLLECTIONS

Cabinets can be exciting. They offer so many collection possibilities. They can be open or closed and they can hold a variety of items. They can also be used for display purposes or strictly for security. Items in a vault can be considered similar to a cabinet collection. Below are examples of cabinet collections that can be found in many homes:

 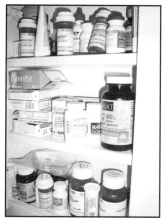 

As with closet collections, cabinet collections may or may not contain like items, although certain types of cabinets usually abide by their intended nature, such as the medicine cabinet collection.

SHELF COLLECTIONS

Shelf collections are often subsets of larger closet or cabinet collections and can maintain unique collection structures unto themselves. In the following images, we offer a variety of shelf collections that can be seen around the house, but probably not yours.

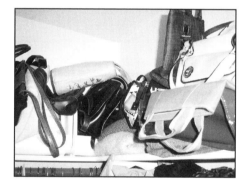

The shelf and its size and location will often dictate how the collection of items will be placed on it, but not always. The physical realities of the shelf dictate the outer limits of the collection, though not necessarily the local arrangements of the items within the collection.

CHAIR COLLECTIONS

Chair collections are unique and cannot always be found in a typical home. After all, most of us use chairs for sitting, not storing our collections. But we thought we'd throw in an example anyway.

REFRIGERATOR COLLECTIONS

We are not positive, but we suspect that refrigerator collections may be unique to Western cultures and perhaps most prevalent in the United States. The refrigerator in many homes acts as a central depository for not only foodstuffs, but also important things to remember. Refrigerator doors can often be considered works of art in themselves by displaying the personalities of the entire household through the images that have been attached. The refrigerator is also unique in that it generally holds two types of collections: the inside collection and the outside collection.

Another aspect of refrigerator collections that make them unique is that there is seemingly no end to the possibilities for structuring the collections both inside and out. Size, color, shape, brand name, food type, container type, nutritional value, ingredients, schedules, to-do list, letters, phone

numbers, photos, magnets, list of recyclables, calendars, notes, what came home most recently, and so on.

PANTRY COLLECTIONS

Not all homes have pantries; however, those that do impose a need on the homeowner to decide what goes in it and how it will be organized. Bottles, boxes, cans, bags, cartons, and other like containers tend to find their way into pantry collections. How they are arranged adds structure to the collection along with other approaches that can add orderliness and the ability to find something when it is needed.

DRAWER COLLECTIONS

The drawer collection is a versatile way of maintaining order for a collection of items in an unordered fashion. Cabinets have drawers, desks have drawers, and you can even get a whole chest of drawers for keeping items organized. In a typical household you may come across drawers filled with silverware sorted by type of utensil, and you may find drawers filled with socks typically paired, but not necessarily. You may also find drawers with other utensils such as pens, pencils, paper clips, rubber bands, and tape. Or you may discover drawers with greeting cards, scratch pads, table linens, or DVDs. The drawer acts as an access point to specific items and may or may not be labeled with that information. In most households drawers are not labeled. The inhabitants remember where collections of things are kept.

Even in large institutional collections, the drawer is an indispensable tool for organizing materials associated with certain types of collections, for example, drawers with gemstones, drawers with insects, drawers with

Make-up drawer

Silverware drawer

photographs, and drawers with unidentifiable pieces of things thought to be ancient or of value.

GARAGE, ATTIC, AND BASEMENT COLLECTIONS

Some might argue that unorganized clutter cannot be considered a structured collection. We beg to differ. Any grouping of items can be considered a collection whether it maintains order or not. The best examples can be seen in most household garages, attics, or basements, where the space is used to collect

items that may not enjoy frequent access or use and are often placed in those locations with a semblance of order based on the space available. Some people are better at organizing and structuring their storage spaces than others. Of course, "better" is a term open to interpretation. It may well be that "I'll put that in the garage until I have to deal with it" is just as useful an organizing guideline as "I'll put this in the optimal place for its intended use."

BOX COLLECTIONS

The box collection is often the most formidable because it is not limited to a specific location in the house. Perhaps they are formal and ubiquitous

because of the uniformity of their shape; especially since the flat tops and bottoms along with perpendicular sides make them so stackable, so nearly gravity-defying. From shoe boxes full of unorganized photographs, to toy boxes, to jewelry boxes, to garages full of storage boxes, the variety of boxed collections is unlimited depending on the nature of the residents and residence.

Coffee Table Collections

The coffee table presents a unique opportunity to display items that are both functional as well as for decorative purposes. In either case the table contents form a collection that can be formally arranged or purposely neglected.

As you can see from these various examples, human beings have a tendency to collect, arrange, organize, and store collections of things. The general nature of those "things" takes on the characteristics of visual objects in the human landscape and presents myriad opportunities for structuring their collection attributes. Collections about the house may be purposeful or the result of gravity, they may be lovely or utilitarian, they may stay "just so" for years or need immediate attention, but nearly all the collections contribute to and are the result of moving through life with a little more ease. To conclude this discussion and move on to how those various collection attributes are derived and used, here are a few more "around the house" collections that many of us take for granted, yet apply structure to every day.

Photos   **Magazines**

Clothes

Linens

Books

Wine

Stuffed animals

Utensils

PART II

THE LANGUAGE OF IMAGE STRUCTURES

We are each incarcerated in our separate perspectives.

M. Merleau-Ponty

As noted in the previous chapters, in the eyes of a beholder, visions are grasped and processed. Processing in the human animal is mostly a conversion to linguistic terms that can be understood in some context, whether it is personal thought or interpersonal communication. In this continuing discussion, we will go to some lengths to provide supporting evidence for the duplicity that often equates language to images, including specific examples of how we tend to describe images as though they were parts of speech. In his book *Semantic Theory*, Kurt Baldinger discusses the relationship of language to concept. We have taken liberties with the book in synthesizing our own view on how language invokes hegemony over images, as indicated in the diagram below.

Applying Language to Visual Experience	Conceptualization in Language B	
Conceptualization in Language A	Language conceptualization in common surrounding a visual experience	Conceptualization surrounding the visual experience unique in Language B
	Conceptualization surrounding the visual experience unique in Language A	Conceptualization independent of a given language

When we speak of images as being worth a thousand words, we tend to lose sight of the fact that often an image can also be a visual event that requires no words at all. We offer as proof the thousands of glances we take during our daily routines to which we give no names, no titles, and no descriptions. The images were there for the seeing, you saw them, and moved on without thinking or saying anything about them. As a further example, we offer in evidence the words of Temple Grandin, an associate professor of animal science at Colorado State University:

> Because I have autism, I live by concrete rules instead of abstract beliefs. And because I have autism, I think in pictures and sounds. I don't have the ability to process abstract thought the way you do. Here's how my brain works: It's like the search engine Google for images. If you say the word "love" to me, I'll surf the Internet inside my brain. Then, a series of images pops into my head. What I'll see, for example, is a picture of a mother horse with a foal, or I think of "Herbie the Lovebug," scenes from the movie *Love Story* or the Beatles song, "Love, love, love."
> (Interview with Temple Grandin, *Morning Edition*, National Public
> Radio, August 14, 2006)

We do not suggest that autism is a prerequisite for being able to conceptualize without language. We do suggest, however, that most of us rely so heavily on language that speaking, communicating, and thinking in pictures is often overlooked as an aspect of the human psyche.

Normal visual experience is a well-balanced event usually composed of seeing, noticing, observing, judging, and appreciating. Seeing is composed of our basic physiological nature that allows us to process light. Noticing is simply a matter of what we choose to give our visual attention. Observing implies prolonged engagement with whatever we are noticing. Up to this point, we have defined visual conceptualization. Once we venture beyond, into the realm of cognitive engagement with the observation, we are at the threshold of language as an application that can add descriptive properties to the observed visual experience. Notice that we called this aspect of the visual engagement "judging," because the visual observation can be either a positive, negative, or neutral experience, depending on the viewer. For example, the visual experience associated with being required to stop at a railroad crossing for an oncoming train. The visual judgment may entail a negative attitude if you are in a hurry to be on time for a scheduled appointment. As such, you may keep looking for the last car of the train so you can continue your journey. Or you find the experience to be a quite relaxed, positive time spent enjoying the respite from your daily chaotic routine as you watch and count the graffiti-covered railcars. In each case, the visual field was the same, but the seeing, noticing, observing, and judgments were different.

Lastly is appreciation. Appreciation, like judgment, is an entirely sub-jective assessment of the viewing experience. However, when language is applied by one viewer and communicated to a second viewer, levels of appreciation can be affected. This act by itself forces a reengagement with the image by the second viewer that once again entails seeing, noticing, observing, and judging. The level of appreciation (attitude toward a viewed image in the context of another point of view) is entirely up to the cognitive mindset of the second viewer. Of note is that these so-called steps are as likely to be parallel events occurring in mere fractions of a second as they are to be sequential viewing activities that often occur when viewing some-thing new or unusual for the first time.

The value of this discussion in the context of image collections and their structure is to point out that image organization is also a process of see-ing, noticing, observing, judging, and appreciating, with each step being as important as the next. Many may argue against our stance regarding these steps; we would prefer to defend it with an example that most readers should appreciate. Our example is an image of a sunset.

Without taking the following visual steps, the language of description and, ultimately of the image collection structure, may suffer.

1. Seeing	The overall panorama (visual field) encompassed by the setting sun, with no attention to detail.
2. Noticing	The elements that enable focal engagement: colors, shapes, textures, size, location, depth of field.
3. Observing	Prolonged focal attention directed at one or several of the noticed elements in the field of vision.
4. Judging	An assignment of applicable language values, including an assessment of the visual experience as a summation of 1, 2, and 3, usually engendering attitudinal overtones (emotion). In essence, the viewer's most fitting description based on both knowledge and past viewing experience: "That is one of the most beautiful sunsets I've ever seen."
5. Appreciating	The nature of an image's description, resulting from shared communication about the viewing experience. "Maybe it's not the 'most' beautiful someone else has seen."

While language may act as a powerful tool for describing and/or explaining an image, it can only emerge after seeing, noticing, and observing have taken place. By the way, did you see, notice, and observe that the sunset photo is grayscale and upside down?

CHAPTER FOUR

IMAGE SEMANTICS: HOW WE DESCRIBE WHAT WE SEE

PHOTOCUTIONARY ACTS

While we do not mean to ignore or eliminate painted images and sculpted images from our discussion of image collections, much of this discussion is centered on photographs. This photocentricity seems warranted even by the numbers. An enormous number of people in the world are making billions of photographs each year. Most of these pictures are in a digital form.

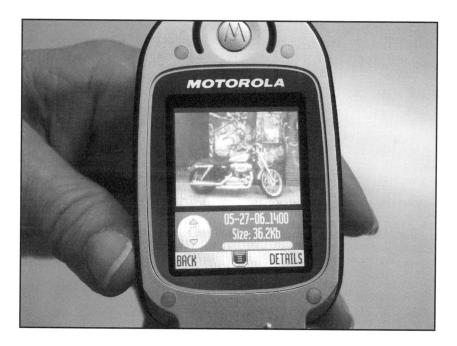

As one focal point for some of the image collection concepts we seek to address, we have modeled, in the spirit of J. L. Austin, "photocutionary behaviors." Austin modeled speech acts as "illocutionary acts." One might summarize his work by saying: "to say something is to do something."

With *photocutionary behaviors* we mean to look at the "doing of something" with photographs. The "doing" of a photocutionary behavior holds whether one is making a quick snapshot with a point-and-shoot camera, using a camera built into a cell phone, or making a sophisticated studio image with a computer-controlled camera costing more than many automobiles. The term holds whether one is making a simple recording or a highly modulated image. What is done at the time of the making of the photograph is irrelevant, as is what is done after the photograph is taken. Of course, doing does not necessarily stop after the image is made. Even in the case of the immediately deleted snapshot, the deletion is the doing of something, though if may well be the limiting case.

We might model photocutionary acts in the following way. A person considers making a photograph. The purpose is irrelevant for our discussion. It might be a snapshot of a child, an elaborate advertising photo, a documentary photo of teens using drugs, or a carefully crafted cityscape.

Austin says of illocutionary acts that they are generally accomplished in order to "persuade, suggest, demand, or promise"; Pratt suggests that documents are constructed in order to accomplish a similar set of goals: "motivate, articulate, educate, or felicitate." To Pratt's list we add "to remember." We quote Oliver Wendell Holmes, to make the case for remembering: "[a photograph] retain [s the subject's] impress, and [later] a fresh sunbeam lays this on the living nerve as if it were radiated from the breathing shape," it would seem not unreasonable to make the overt addition to these lists "to remember." This person making the photograph or, in the case of some complex imaging projects, the person's agents, must engage some instrumentality. Ordinarily this would be a camera in the ordinary sense. Ordinarily, the instrument would be a single camera. In some circumstances there will be lights, a selection of lenses, and postproduction hardware.

The product of the photographic process is an image in some physical form. For much of the history of photography, the immediate product was visible to the eye as a negative or "reversal positive," with subsequent operations producing tangible and manageable prints.

Nowadays the images are likely to be physical only in the sense of arrangements of

bits in some digital storage medium. These may be made manifest as prints, occasional viewings on the cell phone screen, closely scrutinized images on a computer monitor, large-scale prints, or bits analyzed digitally with no human eyes involved in the process.

We might refer to the print or digital file as the "message" or, perhaps for clarity, the "photo message." *Message* is used here in the sense of the substrate modulated to encode some information. In the Shannon and Weaver sense, we distinguish between the message and any meaning it might have for the photographer or for any other viewer. The message may be in a format that is interpretable by others or not; it may be in its original state or not; it may be made with production methods hospitable to subsequent uses or not. Subsequent users may or may not include the name of the original photographer.

Any subsequent use or interpretation of the photo may or may not have a direct relation to the original meaning embodied by the original message of the photo. The persons or objects in front of the lens may or may not be known to the subsequent user. That user may or may not be concerned that the original meaning of the message has not survived. The subsequent user may or may not use the image according to the image (message) maker's original intent.

If we return to our original definition by saying that photocutionary behaviors relate to the "doing of something" with photographs, then such behaviors entail both original and subsequent actions surrounding those photos. The initial photocutionary behavior encompasses the construction of the photo message; yet secondary photocutionary behaviors can entail any other "doing of something" with that photo message (image).

SEEING, NAMING, THINKING

We can see without naming what we see; however, we cannot think about what we see without characterizing that cognitive experience through language. The naming of images and any objects associated with them establishes strands of meaning that can be communicated to others. The problems that exist in structuring names associated with image content and collection structure stem from the naming protocols and categories that are implemented. These problems are inherent in the structure of an image and in both the physical and mental states of a viewer, as in the list below.

The Image

- Content (types of objects)
- Arrangement (of objects)
- Complexity (number of objects in the visual field)
- Spatial organization (depth and distance of objects)
- Physical properties (e.g., colors, shadows, brightness, contrasts)

The Viewer

- Physical:
  - Vantage point (position of the viewer in relation to the image)

- o Visual focus (number of eye movements needed to grasp meaning from the image)
- Mental:
  - o Significance of the image (level of viewer interest)
  - o Utility of viewing the image (functional importance to the viewer)
  - o Value derived from the visual experience (level of needs satisfied)

In concert with the above factors, image creators, image collectors, and image viewers assign words to images. These words tend to be categorical, in the sense that they represent classes of things that share common attributes with other like things so that one image or groups of images can be differentiated from another image or group of images. Over time, the literature has been particularly sensitive to this issue since, for the most part, we speak about images using words, not using other images.

It is important to note, however, that there were brief periods in history when a viewing /speaking overlap occurred; that is, images spoke for themselves before they were spoken about. First was during the period 25,000 to 35,000 years ago, when images appeared on cave walls but the ability to speak in an intelligible language regarding those images was either limited or nonexistent. Second was the period from 1910 to 1930, which encompassed not only taking the still image and adding movement, but also introducing color to formerly only black-and-white images and sound to "go along with" the images being viewed. During that period the viewing public had exposure to all of the following: silent black-and-white films, silent color films, black-and-white films with dialogue, and color films with dialogue. The question arises: Were the silent images viewed and interpreted with the same meaning as the language-driven images? Without superfluous dramatics on this point, we will simply defer to Sergei Eisenstein, director of the First Moscow Worker's Theatre in 1922, who said: "Sound meant the subversion of montage." With the juxtaposing of image and sound (language), Eisenstein felt that the viewer's focus was no longer on the visual message but was transferred to the spoken word, which resulted in sublimating the image (the montage or film sequence) and the strictly visual meanings or meanings that could be derived from the images alone.

The value of stating this point of view relates directly to the structure of image collections, because the factors described as viewing problems, mentioned above, combine with language factors that can contribute to subverting image meaning instead of inducing clarity for the viewer. These problems have been stated in a variety of ways and depend on the mode of research and discipline within which they have been posed, which include, but are not limited to, the following.

BASIC, SUBORDINATE, AND SUPERORDINATE LEVELS OF CATEGORIZATION

In a series of psychological experiments in the 1970s, Eleanor Rosch argued that when people name an object, they rely on cognitive economy derived from cues (image attributes) offered from an image to place that object in some *basic* category that is linguistically useful. Rosch further divided these levels of visual categorization into the *superordinate* level that contains or categorizes the basic-level object as well as a host of other objects that have some particular attribute(s) in common; for example, *car* is a basic-level category of the superordinate category *transportation*. Rosch would argue that upon seeing the image below, a viewer would more likely respond to the image at the basic level of car than refer to it as transportation.

Rosch further extended the idea to a third level which she defined as the subordinate level of categorization where a viewer is likely to respond with a category that has fewer attributes in common than either the basic or superordinate categories of the same object. Thus, a viewer possessing specific knowledge may refer to the photo above as a Volkswagen or even a Beetle. At this subordinate level, while the term is intended to more clearly define the image object, the naming of it introduces yet another problem of using words for images. For example, at the time of this writing, using the term *beetle* in the Google Internet search engine provided no less than 358,000 images, of which the first ten images included five Volkswagen Beetles and five insect beetles.

The crux of the underlying problem is more appropriately resolved as an exercise in psycholexicology, as put forth by George Miller and Phillip Johnson-Laird in their 1976 publication, *Language and Perception*. They state that "the existence in English of such a general word as *thing* means that there is some label you can apply to every concrete object, even when you are uncertain about the applicability of a more specific label."

Many image collections, both public and private, are structured around this type of *superordinate, basic, and subordinate* categorization. For example, art in the J. Paul Getty Museum's online collection is divided first into the superordinate categories of artists, types of art, and subjects. The basic-level categories under Types of Art include architecture, decorative objects, drawings, furniture, costumes, manuscripts, paintings, photographs, and sculpture, and the subordinate categories under Painting include landscapes, myths and stories, portraits, real life, religion, and still lifes.

At the outset, this approach appears to be a logical solution, giving the curators opportunities to organize the images for display and giving patrons functional access for viewing the categories and specific works within categories. However, access to the actual work of art and access to an online image of the work pose two different issues in relation to collection structure. The actual physical work cannot hang in two places at once, even though it may fit into more than one category; whereas an online image can occupy and be viewed under several different categories by representing it more than once.

Decisions must be made as to where the work will be hung on display and where it will appear in an online format. For this example, we refer to the Getty holdings known as portraits of Pope Gregory XV and Pope Clement VII. An assumption for one who has never been to the Getty Museum is that these works would be on display in a gallery of portraits, since Portraits was one of the categories used to describe the online collection. However, the museum as a functioning institution has decided to further subdivide the collection into chronological components using pavilions. The galleries at the Getty are housed in five pavilions, none of which conforms to the superordinate, basic, or subordinate categories of the online image collection. The pavilions are categorized as North, East, South, West, and Exhibitions. So if we were looking for the portraits of the popes mentioned above, without asking for directions, where should we look?

We are told online that the North Pavilion holds paintings and sculptures dating up to 1600 and that the East Pavilion features primarily seventeenth-century Baroque art, including Dutch, French, Flemish, and Spanish paintings. The South Pavilion houses eighteenth-century paintings, and the West Pavilion features sculpture, Italian decorative arts of the 1700s through 1900, and nineteenth-century paintings. In essence, the structure of the physical collection is different from that of the online collection. As such, a potential viewer of the physical collection must have knowledge that is different from that needed to find an image in the online collection. With the information gleaned from the online pages for each portrait (Pope Clement VII, painted about 1531, and Pope Gregory XV, painted about 1622), we suspect that the former would be in the North Pavilion and the latter in the East Pavilion.

Turning our attention to the Getty online collection, we observe that although each pope appears in the portrait category, neither image appears in the religion category. And we further note that several portraits, including a work titled *Portrait of a Canon*, appeared in the religion category but not in the portrait category. Let us clarify. This is not a critique or a criticism of the Getty Museum's collection and organization. We use this example only to point out some of the language difficulties inherent in structuring an image collection that may often work to the detriment of the patron or viewer of the images in such a collection.

With this somewhat brief outline, it is apparent that structures of image collections can take on a variety of formats even when the images in question remain the same. The question we pose is: Which naming protocols and categorization formats are more conducive for viewer access to image collections, and do such protocols and formats actually exist?

ICONOGRAPHY

For an answer, we could point to the earlier work of Erwin Panofsky, who, in an attempt to define meaning in the visual arts, suggested that images can be viewed at three levels of understanding, which include the preiconographic, the iconographic, and the iconology levels. Although his focus was on the fine arts, these somewhat esoteric terms speak to the same issue of naming images, in that the preiconographic level of image understanding is suggested to be the simple statements of fact that a viewer can derive from an image, which coincides with Rosch's later-defined "basic" level of image viewing. In Panofsky's terms, the same image of the Volkswagen Beetle could be considered as including preiconographic terms such as car, blue, street, and building. In other words, it is what it is.

Panofsky would likely have moved to the iconographic level of description by addressing some sort of theme engendered by the image, such as "parked in the driveway"; and lastly, Panofsky's iconology of the image would encompass an interpretation of why the image exists that may or may not include where and when the image was created, why it was created from this particular vantage point, and what the image may mean from a cultural and/or historical perspective. Of course, our descriptions of these are ordinarily verbal and may or may not adequately represent the mental engagement of the photographer, subject, or subsequent viewer; but they may be of some use. Such descriptive information for this image could include the following:

- Mary owned an early VW Beetle in the 1960s
- Good gas mileage
- New house
- Expounding on 1960s with son
- Teaching son to drive stick shift car

OFNESS AND ABOUTNESS

As the capacity to handle and manage digital image collections improved throughout the 1980s and 1990s, it was soon recognized that the more traditional or conventional methods for classifying, indexing, and cataloguing image collections posed a multitude of issues for trying to make those collections more easily accessible to online viewers. The most prominent of those issues was, and is, as you might suspect from the preceding, how to effectively assign words to images to facilitate storing, seeking, and retrieving to achieve the greatest efficiency. Professionals across a variety of disciplines have identified that managing collections of images, whether in physical or virtual environments, involves a different realm of cognitive scrutiny than managing documents that involve textual material only. Quotes on this subject are varied and abundant, so it should not be considered arrogant to add our own:

> Because the attributes of an image are different from the attributes of a text-based document, the methods that are used for accessing, storing, and retrieving images, of necessity, must also be different ... even if words are used.

Literature on image classification that appeared in the late 1980s asserted that what is objectively depicted in an image is the "ofness" associated with that image, whereas that which the image subjectively represents can be considered the "aboutness" associated with that same image. From a semantic point of view, we might say that an image's *ofness* is what it specifies (the specifics made available in the visual field), and an image's *aboutness* is what it concerns (what it relates to, as derived from the Latin "to sift together"). Returning to the image of our Volkswagen Beetle, we could say that its ofness is a "car on the street," whereas its aboutness is "living in north Texas in the late 1990s."

From an image collection point of view, most private collections include labels that name the images in the collection as a function of image ofness, which equates to Rosch's basic level and Panofsky's iconographic level of image description. Examples might include a stamp collection, a postcard collection, a collection of photographs, or a cave painting image collection. Our message in this publication is that whatever the approach to naming images in a collection, it usually involves some basic, iconographic ofness associated with each image in the collection.

In the public sector, however, the process of naming a collection is not so straightforward, because oftentimes the structure of the collection is actually a collection of collections, which tends to force the introduction of some superordinate name for the overarching characteristics of the collection grouping.

For example, a trip across the United States would afford viewing opportunities of image collections in almost every major city in museums of art, science, and natural history, and with none of these words giving us an indication of what is included in any of the collections; but they give us a fairly good idea of what is not included. In contrast, if we came across the American Museum of Fly Fishing in Manchester, Vermont, we most likely would have a good understanding regarding both the *ofness* (specifics) and the *aboutness* (related to) surrounding the structure of the collection before walking in the door.

IMPROPER NOUNS

This is not to say that the only way to describe a collection is based on the above theoretical frameworks. A recent search of the publicly accessible images on the Flickr Web site (www.flickr.com) found a collection of no less than 23,950 photos of "me," none of which were, in fact, me. We also did a similar search for "you" and found 9,787 images, none of which were you (even though you have 127 photos of yourself on the Flickr website). And another search for the word "Washington," using the Yahoo image search engine, found a collection of over 4.5 million images with basic-level, iconographic depictions of and about Washington, which included the following as part of the first page of twenty images: George Washington, Denzel Washington, Mount Washington, map of Washington (state), photo from Iraq (*Washington Post*), Washington Square, The Capitol (Washington, D.C.), Washington Crosses the Delaware, map of Washington, D.C. These search results, and most likely millions more using thousands of keywords and keyword combinations, point to the dilemma of structuring an image collection for the purpose of efficient and effective storage, viewing, and retrieval.

SUBJECT HEADINGS

Up to this point, we have not discussed the concept of an image title. Many image collections are structured around the titles that the creator of the image or collector of the image has assigned to it. By using tools such as *Library of Congress Subject Headings* (LCSH), along with the narrow terms,

broad terms, and related terms associated with those headings, authorities managing large image collections have attempted to approach image labeling, but not without forfeiting other attributes of an image that are not contained in the multivolume list of headings. While the word *forfeit* may seem a bit harsh for those who have spent hundreds of hours organizing images in the *LOC Subject Headings*, our contention is that the naïve viewers of images in such collections are most likely to describe them in basic-level or iconographic terms. For example, returning once again to our image of the "blue car parked in the driveway" or "blue car parked on the street," the image by those titles would not be easily found in a collection structured around the LCSH. The word *blue* is not a heading, but it does occur as a narrower topic under colors. The word *car* also is not a subject heading, but Cars (Automobiles), Classic cars, Compact cars, Economy cars, Foreign cars, Midget cars, Small cars, Street-cars, Used cars, and Vintage cars are all available for identifying this image. Which one would you use?

If we return to the fact that what we see is not always what we say about what we see, *subject headings* may or may not work for a large variety of images (totaling in the millions) that are part of both small and large collections.

Recognizing this problem, library and like-minded professionals have sought to enhance the naming protocols associated with describing images by introducing other tools to aid in storing and retrieving images in library or museum-like collections. Such tools include the *Union List of Artist Names* (ULAN), the *Getty Thesaurus of Geographic Names* (TGN), the *Art & Architecture Thesaurus* (AAT), and the Iconclass system, all of which are structured naming protocols designed to improve access to information about art, architecture, and material culture. While these tools may be too burdensome for the private collector of images, they have also placed burdens on those who structure large collections, because each of these systems, in its own way, cannot encompass a vocabulary that is extensive enough to provide adequate descriptive information or points of image engagement for every viewer.

The semantics of an image, in essence, consists of a mental triumvirate composed of words that have meaning for an originator, an owner, and a viewer of an image object. The efficacy of those words for achieving efficient and effective image collection structure, however, resides with the nature of language, not with the nature of vision.

CAN WE THINK WITH OUR EYES?

It was Cezanne who identified the painter's task as one that includes *penser avec les yeux*—"to think with the eyes." Although humans have used their visual faculties for thousands of years, it was not until the French Impressionists took a stand in the world of art in 1874 to emphasize that how people look and think about images extends beyond mere objectivity. The Impressionists no longer spoke about the subjects of their work; their concern was the "motif," or thematic elements that defined the work.

Today, as we note the proliferation of digital image databases, we can also note that the predominant approaches for efficient and effective image access and retrieval from such databases have centered on object-based indexing methodologies, the focus being on the subject, not on the motif. Just as the young Impressionists were confronted with narrow and conservative attitudes about their art, so are today's organizers of image collections constrained by traditional approaches that limit the extent to which image viewers are able to think with their eyes. The Impressionists all agreed that a picture should present only the image that struck the painter's eye at the moment of painting. Only what one saw, not what one knew to be there, was their intent. In turn, viewers of images should be able to explicate their impressions of what they see, not just what is there, by object, by title, or by a mechanized extraction of content. And, if viewers are given such cognitive rights, then those same rights should be given to those others later looking to retrieve such images of those objects or qualities. If impressions are the fruits of visual thinking, then no attempts to technically reduce such notions to thesaurus or subject headings could ever encompass the richness of human induction when exposed to an image. No individual or group of individuals, no matter how professional or rule-intensive the approach, could ever capture a full panoply of impressions invoked by an image.

Thinking with one's eyes is a process of reconceptualization and, as such, represents a cognitive system that seeds a variety of possible representations that engenders a rich palette of diverse terms. The current widespread dissemination and use of images, especially in digital formats, urges examination of this integrated process of perception and cognition to gain a better understanding of how individuals make their own juxtapositions about and between images. Although technology has served to advance the cause of more opportunities to create images, both by professionals and the public at large, the creation of effective underlying technologies for organizing, storing, and accessing those images has become a more tedious and overwhelming task.

CAN WE SEE WHAT WE'RE NOT SEEING?

In contrast to text, one difficulty encountered in classifying and categorizing images from an objective perspective is determining what the image conveys

to the viewer. Objects, features of objects, and labels for aggregations of objects in a collection may fail to convey the same meaning across all viewing audiences. For example, when the following image was presented to a group of viewers, it was interpreted descriptively as forest, jungle, or beach.

A Word about Prototypes

Such interpretations by image viewers have a tendency to confound attempts at organizing image collections in a way that would convey the same meanings to all viewers of the collection contents. Thus most formal collections as well as those maintained for personal use tend to use the broadest terminology for describing the collection content. This general characteristic for naming image collections points to an underlying cognitive need for knowing what is being viewed without concern for prototypical displacement. For example, when confronted with an opportunity to see an "art" collection, the unsuspecting viewer will already have an existing prototype for the word *art* already in mind, which will, for the most part, be construed as an opportunity to see some creative works that are drawn, painted, sculpted, or constructed or that are displayed artifacts from some particular time or place. Hence, prototypes used for descriptive reference act as labels that define a set of features that can separate one image from another or one collection from another, such as a museum of "modern" art.

However, when we speak of "prototypical displacement" and its impact on collection viewers, we are referring to the greater need for clarity while viewing, browsing, or searching through the whole collection. For example, the viewer already understands that the viewing experience entails seeing objects of art, but has no interest in anything other than seeing examples of French Impressionism. Will examples of French Impressionism be available for viewing in a venue described as housing "modern" art? We now have an example of prototypical displacement: Is French Impressionism considered to be modern art? For some the answer is yes, and for others the answer is no. As image viewers, we each maintain a cognitive prototype for the meaning of modern art.

Exemplars

To extend this discussion and its impact on collection structure, we refer back to the image that was described as depicting a forest, a jungle, and a beach by different viewers. Why do we get different descriptions? The image was a static representation of a group of objects; however, the visual representation of the objects in the photo presented to viewers had features that represented exemplars to the viewers, causing interpretations that differed from viewer to viewer. One viewer saw a group of trees. For that viewer a group of trees represents a forest. Another viewer saw that the trees were of a particular type that, for that viewer, was an exemplar of a jungle. Another viewer's attention was guided to the ground beneath the trees, which appeared to be sand and thus an exemplar of a beach.

Our objective to this point is to present the reader with a clear understanding of why images cannot be clearly understood. An image is always open to interpretation, and those interpretations are often a function of the prototypes and exemplars that viewers bring to the viewing experience. Hence, structuring collections is at minimum a twofold process:

1. What is in the collection? What should it be called?
2. How do the items in the collection need to be grouped (categorized)?

We would further argue that without both elements there is no collection structure. If the first questions are absent, there is no cohesion, which results in simply an aggregation of disparate groups of items.

If question 2 is missing, there is no organization, which results in a random sampling of items. Take for example a personal collection of photographs. It may be called a family collection of photos; however, if the photos are not organized, it is only an aggregation of family photos, but it is by no means a structured collection. Likewise, if the photos are neatly organized by time, date, event, people in the photographs, or other organizing categories, it also may not be a structured collection because it has no nominal designation, such as a collection of photos taken by me, or a collection of my family photos, or a collection of photos from the 1990s.

To repeat, structuring a collection requires at least two steps:

1. Giving it a name
2. Organizing the items within it

While this may sound elementary and simplistic, these are very difficult tasks to perform if the collection is going to be viewed by others, and even more difficult if viewers are given the right to access (find) something they specifically need within the collection. If you remain somewhat skeptical, put down the book and go find the photos of your child blowing out the candles on his or her birthday cake. Yes, we mean all of them. Oh! You didn't organize your collection that way. Then I guess you'll need to read the rest of the book.

CHAPTER FIVE

IMAGE SEMIOTICS: HOW WE DESCRIBE WHAT WE DON'T SEE

T HE PREVIOUS DISCUSSION may be quite appropriate for describing images in a collection where the "knowledge" of the viewer is a correlate to those images. Often, however, the image seeker or image viewer experiences a cognitive disconnect with an image being viewed, resulting in what we choose to call "crippled viewer syndrome." The nature of this crippling effect when one is viewing an image can be described in terms of its semiotics.

By definition, *semiotics* is the study of sign systems by which meaningful communication occurs. Its modern history resides in the works of Charles S. Peirce, Ferdinand de Saussure, and Roland Barthes. For our purposes, semiotics has a direct connection to image collection structure, because image viewers often do not know the meaning of what they see; yet they know what they are looking at. For example, let us direct your attention to the photograph without providing any information about it and pose these questions:

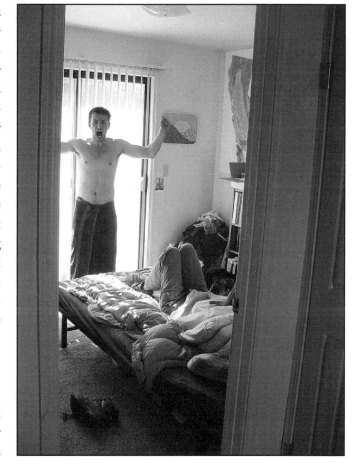

1. What do you see?
2. What does it mean?

You are now well practiced in semiotics. This particular photo is composed of objects that represent signs that signify some meanings that in some way establish meaning for the image viewer. If the viewer does not know what the signs signify, then crippled viewer syndrome sets in. An interesting aspect of crippled viewer syndrome is that it does not produce the same symptoms across all sufferers. In this instance, the second author of this book took the photo, so he knows exactly what this image means (stands for). The first author of this book knows what this image means because he has been told. Each reader of this book will structure a meaning for this photo which may or may not be "correct." However, the correctness is an issue that may or may not be of concern only to the image creator. Any readers of this book who view this image can have a very intelligent discussion with each other and will most likely agree on their answers to question 1. However, it is most unlikely that readers' answers to question 2 will correspond to each other.

Let us, for the moment, take this discussion into the public arena of art, science, and history museum collections. How often do visitors see images on display but do not know what they signify? The seasoned professional will quickly retort that written descriptions and the more recent informational audiophones are provided to patrons specifically for the purpose of giving meaning to the image objects on display. We have no argument with those improvements; however, if a patron has not seen the image, has not read the description or heard the audiotape, how could someone without that information find or even describe that same visual experience unless they stumbled across it? And secondly, does "knowing about" always enhance the experience of "looking at"?

A third term that acts as a signpost for semiotics is symbolism. In semiotics, a symbol is a sign that signifies something other than itself and has no resemblance to the sign. In contrast to the world of words, the world of vision has myriad signs that act as symbols of some sort or another, which is why images are so difficult to identify beyond just describing their signs. For example, religious art and a variety of more recent art movements are filled with signs that symbolize something else and thus provide meaning that goes beyond what is seen in the image. Without the knowledge necessary to interpret the meaning of the symbols, the viewer of such images is left with crippled viewer syndrome and can only think of and discuss the image in terms of the signs it contains. Imagine being given an opportunity to view the twelfth-century bestiary housed in the British Library. How many animals could you name? How many meanings for those animals could you describe?

Which brings us to the fourth important term associated with semiotics: *codes*. Codes establish rules for transmitting the intended meanings in the most effective way. In our example above, a bestiary served as a book of codes that described not only the animal signs (that is, lamb, lion, etc.), but what the sign symbolized (meek, strong, etc.). Take another look at the previous image from a semiotic point of view. How many signs do you see? What, if anything, do these signs symbolize? And are those symbols part of a conventional code (socially, culturally, historically, etc.)?

THOUGHTS FROM THE PHOTOGRAPHER (O'CONNOR)

On the face of it, this photograph is rather unremarkable. A young man is captured acting like a young man, perhaps before or after a shower, if we look at the towel. The resolution of the image is actually fairly low by any modern standards; the composition would not earn high marks in a photography course, for the door casing occupies essentially half of the image real estate and we do not see the young man's right arm. There is another pair of legs in the image, but the head of the person on the bed is obscured by the door. The image that is unremarkable in the technical or compositional sense is quite remarkable in another sense. This is a photograph of my son (Brian) a few years ago. The photograph enables me to see the way he looked on that day. This is no small feat.

This image is remarkable in another way that relates directly to image collections. Some time ago I was invited to hang a show of my photographs. The images were all to be printed on one forty-foot long sheet of photographic print paper so that they would present a holistic display and so viewers could write comments in the margins. The collection of images would be

drawn from a collection of one hundred images I was considering for the show. The entire collection of one hundred was first presented to the owner of the coffee shop and gallery so that he might deselect any images that might be disturbing to viewers and, thus, bad for business.

This image is one of only two images that were deselected. Those not deselected—put out of the collection—included a dead mouse in a trap, an IV needle in the arm of an elderly woman, and a discreet nude photograph of a woman. The earlier photograph of my son was rejected because of the "overt sexuality" of the image. When I explained that the subject was my son

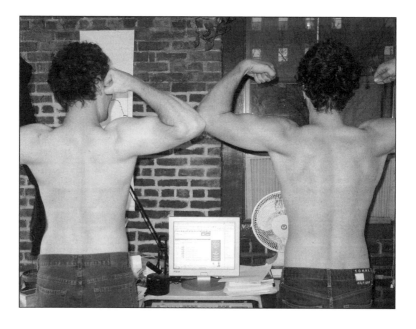

after surfing, the legs of the woman on the bed were brought up. I explained that the legs were those of his mother—this was even worse. To some degree, rightfully, the owner said that no clues pointed to the people being my son and wife and that the framing by the door made this almost a voyeuristic image.

Intriguingly, the second image rejected from the collection was an image of our two sons because it appeared (to the shop-gallery owner) "too gay." Here we are confronted with the specificity of photographs; the very quality that makes them so powerful as memory aids can also leave them bereft of context and open to interpretations in one collection that would never hold in another. As a part of the functional environment, this photograph pre-

This is not a pipe.

sented to one set of eyes (mine) a cool image of my sons in 2002—the result of a photocutionary act on my part. As a part of the functional environment for another set of eyes, with no knowledge of the circumstances of production, there was only a two-dimensional projection of two young, muscled men that was, if not iconic for homosexuality, at least interpretable as such.

This discussion on semiotics and the questions it has posed point to how we use language to say something other than what we see. This concept is not new and has been pervasive throughout the research literature in varieties of attempts to formulate the most efficacious approach to image access, especially in online database settings. Many of these approaches have been discussed in this and prior chapters; however, another issue that has not been articulated relates to our own linguistic legacy of confounding terminology. We can talk about "things" in a variety of ways; some are accurate, some are not accurate, and others lie somewhere in between. An image can withstand all varieties of descriptive narrative. Painter René Magritte is an excellent example, with titles such as *The Red Model*, *The Lovers*, and *This Is Not a Pipe*.

Most image collections are structured around "it is" commentaries, whereas most image seekers and viewers will come across an image and say: "It looks like _____." These two approaches are not always compatible and can play havoc with image search and retrieval capabilities. Simile is only one of several language conundrums that can take a sign and turn it into a symbol whose code may reside only with the viewer, not with the image collection and its structure. Some of these other language barriers (or access points) to images through words include metaphor, allegory, hyperbole, irony, metonymy, anachronism, synecdoche, and litotes.

METAPHOR

One thing described as if it were another. For example, if life is just a bowl of cherries, can I use the keyword "life" to access an image of a bowl of cherries? We can generate images that might express metaphors, but the difficulties in describing an image as metaphorical are significant. The literary metaphor simply may not translate the image realm.

Let us conduct a thought experiment. If the phrase "is a" appears in a

sentence (for example, Life is a bowl of cherries, All the world is a stage, or It is a dog's life), then look up the definitions of the nouns on either side of the phrase "is a." If the definition of one noun does not contain the other, then there is a reasonable chance that a metaphor is present. What does an image seeker do then to detect the metaphorical image? Using one of the above examples, what set of RGB values (red, green, blue) and edges in a photograph of a stage would tell a viewer that the image is not contained within the image definition of "world" and is, therefore, only a metaphor for the world?

ALLEGORY

A visible symbol representing an abstract idea. *The Four Continents*, a painting by Peter Paul Rubens housed in the Kunsthistorisches Museum, Vienna, could be considered an example of how each of the image objects in the painting are symbols for four continents of the world, yet there are no continents in the painting.

In the photograph of the Statue of Liberty reproduction, we are presented with a symbol of freedom that does not necessarily project that concept unless the viewer is familiar with the object in front of the lens. Indeed, this image was actually made as a part of a series to project a rather different concept—faux reality. Anybody familiar with the original statue would likely know that this would be an impossible view of the statue.

HYPERBOLE

Used to heighten effect, catalyze recognition, or create a humorous perception. For example, if I'm so hungry I could eat a horse, then I should be able to use the keyword "hungry" to retrieve images of horses. Actual hyperbole within an image is a problematic concept, though perhaps the repetition of some element, as in the "Caution Beware Of" image, could be said to be hyperbolic. So, too, might be the presentation of a portrait with the skin color given a high red value to represent "I was so embarrassed my face was beet red." Though in these examples there is still a requirement for some external understanding. An image of a set of universal negation signs would not be said to be hyperbolic if it were just in a helpful hints article, even if there were more of them than in the beach warning.

Perhaps a collage of images could be used to heighten effect. That is, perhaps a collage could be said to be a photographic form of the production

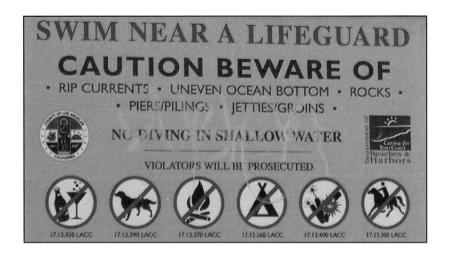

of hyperbole rather than a mere reproduction of some other occurrence of hyperbole. In the collage of images made from frames of motion picture film of a women's track meet, the agglomeration of images, the use of details and whole bodies, and the inclusion of frames that show artifacts of motion are all intended to give the sense of power, determination, and speed inherent in the participants' perception of the event.

IRONY

A misleading use of a visual image to present one thing to the viewer, but actually representing the opposite. It is something to make a photograph of something ironic, such as "Fire Line" stretched at a flooded river. It is quite another to place descriptors of the irony into an access system. The "Fire Line" photograph was happened upon, whereas the "Art of Shaving" photograph was purposely constructed. However, even the shaving image is not photographically ironic; that is, it is not some sense of lighting or color that is intrinsically ironic. Imagine attempting to find an ironic picture—what would you type into a search engine?

METONYMY

Using the name of one thing for that of another of which it is an attribute or with which it is associated. For example, to illustrate "The pen is mightier than the sword," we may not necessarily be looking for images of pens or swords, but we may be looking for images of peace treaties and military equipment. For example, the Iron Curtain guard tower on the Austria/Hungary border looks tiny here, perhaps giving the appearance of insignificance in light of new political realities.

ANACHRONISM

Something placed in an inappropriate period in time. One might assert that anachronism doesn't play a role in image retrieval as most of the other issues do. However, how often do curators of large collections and private collectors of small collections struggle with the dates that an image was created, purchased, sold, etc. in trying to maintain or improve the accuracy of the collection-related data or keep the collection in proper chronological order? Often, image viewers don't care.

Here is a modern photograph of an antique ship, now no longer rigged with hemp rope—a subtle anachronism. The less subtle anachronism, however, is the flag with fifty stars and the background items that are of modern manufacture. In one sense, the use of a digital imaging system to render a full sixteen-million-color image of a nineteenth-century vessel might be said to be a photographic anachronism.

We might turn this idea on its head and, in so doing, have an example of a photographic analog to verbal anachronism. We might take an image in modern time and purposely "antique" the look. Here we have an image of a Colt .45 Border Patrol revolver that is a genuine antique firearm. Photographing it with a digital camera in full color renders a fair representation of the gun as it looks today. Yet, if we want a photograph of an antique weapon with an antique look, we can desaturate the image, leaving only a gray-scale photograph that would be more appropriate to the photographic look of the days when the pistol was new. However, we still have a problem with regard to searching in a collection. How is one to search for a photograph of an object using a search term such as "antique look"? Using the eye-brain system to rapidly scan pho-

tos for the antique look might be one component of a solution. What would an antique look be? Would that be the lack of color or the background elements? Would an actual antique gun set beside a laptop computer be an antique look?

SYNECDOCHE

A part of something substituted for the whole, such as a set of wheels, or wheels being a reference to a car. We went to the FreeFoto.com Web site and entered the keyword "wheels" and saw only two cars in the first 500 photos of the 921 available for viewing. The obvious assumption by the developers of the FreeFoto image database is that if we wanted images of cars we would have entered "car" or "cars" as our search criteria, not "wheels." We consider that to be an erroneous consideration when structuring an image collection. The image of the slot machine payout line might be used to illustrate the phrase "wheel of fortune." Of course, such a use

requires an understanding of two variations of the word *fortune* and an understanding that predigital slot machines display their numbers on wheels. A recent Google image search for "wheel(s) of fortune" yielded scores of images from the popular television show of that name, a picture of prayer wheels, a poster for a bicycle ride raising money for medical research, a cheese-making company, and even one image of a fortune-telling machine that used three wheels mounted in the same manner as those in the slot machine image, but no slot machine picture.

LITOTES

A calculated understatement. For example, how could an image be described that depicts something that's "not a bad idea"? Using a term such as "good ideas" might not be a bad idea. However, we are left with the problem so prevalent in image searching, of trying to determine just what the image analog of the verbal effect might be. The following photos and commentaries represent how litotes intercedes between the understated visual

effect and the ability to expand that understatement to a meaningful verbal expression.

In this first visual example of litotes, the question mark is an actual object suspended above an information desk. The verbal analog, however, is nowhere to be seen. Only the visual understatement, albeit quite large, is intended to advise the uninformed visitors.

In this second example of litotes, both the visual and the verbal expression are understated by using the initials L.B.J. on a sign quite removed from the object it is describing.

This third example of litotes shows how understated visual effects can often generate an overwhelming abundance of verbal expressions.

The question mark image is an actual documentary recording of people and objects. The question mark is a suspended sculpture. Some of the people in the image had not even noticed it until they were shown the image on the camera's display. People walking beneath a huge question mark and paying no attention seemed to present a form of understatement.

Perhaps photographing a colorful object in gray scale, or framing the primary object of interest by putting a great deal of frame space around it, or selecting a small number of objects from a large field could all be said to be forms of photographic litotes. These images would be litotes only if the effects were calculated. Calculated by whom?

Photographing the statue of Lyndon Johnson on his ranch with a good deal of

frame space and the park sign, "L.B.J. Statue" was intended to understate the importance and stature of a once powerful man within the frame of nature and time. The sign naming the statue occupies more frame real estate than does the statue, trumpeting more than is evident.

Here the spare lines of granite stairs leading to a lake and some dead grass are all that break up a field of snow. The purposeful elimination of the trees around the lake and the bridge just above the frame line were intended to emphasize the concepts of cold and bleak. Perhaps it is worth noting here that much of the history of retrieval systems has been grounded in describing and searching with nouns, yet many potential uses and possible descriptions are adjectival. Again, since photographs are recordings of specific objects made under specific circumstances, it may not always be easy to make the leap from seeking an image of a general concept to just what objects and circumstances might stand for that concept.

PICTURES ARE NOT WORDS

Pictures are not words. That seems self-evident, but it has not been the guiding force for most collection and retrieval design. The object in front of the lens or some more general class to which the object belongs has been the tag, the entry into the collection. In some ways, it could hardly be otherwise. Until recently there was no simple way to search for color, composition, texture, or other image components. These are available now, but there is still no simple way to describe or arrange or search for an image at a level above the image primitive (color, texture, edge) and below or beside the name of the object in front of the lens.

These various parts of speech all point to some of the precautionary measures that bear consideration when structuring a collection of images around language-based vocabularies. Jacques Barzun, in his 1973 lecture on "The Use and Abuse of Art," put forth our argument in more eloquent terms:

> Together with homogenized properties that are indistinguishable Technology has multiplied the product, and those that were once users and choosers have become helpless flood victims. There is too much to sort out, let alone assimilate. And much of what we are able to see is merged.

CHAPTER SIX

IMAGE ENGAGEMENT AND COMPLEXITY

THE STRUCTURE OF an image, the structure of human engagement with an image, and structures of image collections each maintain an integrated set of characteristics that make the eye-mind experience a complex matter involving photocutionary behaviors, as discussed earlier. For this continuing discussion, we define *structure* as something whose parts relate to each other in some pattern of organization. While an image may consist of parts that include its colors, its shapes, and its textures, image structure as a whole relates to how those parts are organized. Most of the images we see already have their parts organized into patterns of color, shape, and texture. A painter, sculptor, photographer, or other craftsman, however, must compose the parts before a structured image appears. The structure that appears may or may not appear the same to all viewers of that image.

This juncture also provides the opportunity to think about the distinction between photographs and paintings, considering that we are using both in our discussions surrounding structures of image collections. Both photographs and paintings present the eye with color, luminance, and edge data, and both present their data in two-dimensional formats. But what distinguishes the two representations? For any individual pair of images—one photograph and one painting—we might say that one captures the details more "faithfully," that is, the one-to-one correspondence between the data points (captured objects and their details) are rendered more accurately by the photographic process than by painting the original scene. However, if both photographic capabilities (optics, sensor characteristics, color management issues, etc.) and painterly capabilities are considered, such an argument may not hold. A prime example might be photorealist painter Robert Bechtle, who presents us with an uncanny reflection of middle-class American culture with his work. Probably the best description of the difference between photographs and paintings was given by the narrative material used by the San Francisco Museum of Modern Art for an exhibition that speaks of Bechtle's work as leaving out just enough detail to remain "painterly." His paintings not only present a photorealistic data set to the eye of the viewer, they also present snapshot images. That is, the subjects are what one would expect of photographic snapshots: family on vacation standing by the station wagon, car sitting in driveway by lawn and house, and so forth.

Even though there are paintings that look photographic and photographs that look painterly, there remains a significant distinction—the photographic image is made by recoverable and repeatable processes. In both the painting and the photograph, light bounces off the surfaces of an object or set of objects, enters a lens, triggers recording processes, and results in an image. In the case of the painter, the resulting image depends on the skill and aesthetic choices of the painter; in the case of the photographer, the resulting image, while influenced by aesthetic choices and technical competence, is the result of optical and electronic (or photochemical) processes. We can recover the optical characteristics of the lens and the electronic characteristics of the sensor and have a record of at least a significant portion of the representational process. While we might have the words of the painter or significant critiques of the painter's work, we can never know with precision what representation rules will be put into place for any particular image.

This is not a trivial argument in light of collection structure, retrieval from a collection, or use of images. Suppose we want to compare Pacific and Atlantic coast seagulls, or build a kayak from an image, or reconstruct a crime or historical scene. We would want to know that color, shape, and edges, and relative distances, could be accurately reconstructed from images of these subjects. It is true that lenses may introduce distortions of lines and colors, but we can know those parameters accurately and correct for them.

In terms of collections, the availability of camera data within the digital files have opened up new forms of collection building. One can now search online photo sites by type of camera used to make the photographs. There is no fundamental reason one could not search by shutter speed, lens length, or even light metering pattern.

Now, the mere fact that representation codes are recoverable from photographs does not make them inherently superior to paintings. Indeed, there are times when one may not want the representational fidelity of a photograph. It is easy to think of portraits in which certain features are diminished or even ignored. Perhaps more significant are instances in which one wants a recording that makes distinctions not evident in visible lighting. For example, medical images may well be more easily read if colors are enhanced or even modified to render separate systems as distinct, even though they exhibit the same color and texture. A watercolor painting made on a visit to a

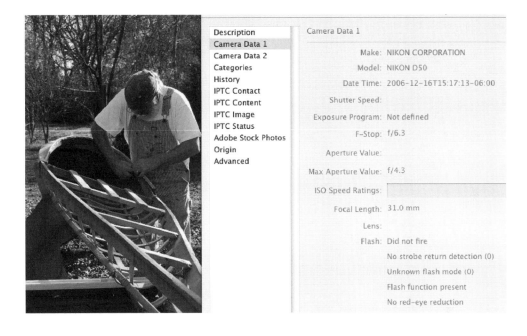

Taken on
February 28, 2007 at 11.29pm PST

Posted to Flickr
March 1, 2007 at 5.05pm PST

Camera:	**Panasonic DMC-FZ15**
Exposure:	**0.006 sec (1/160)**
Aperture:	**f/2.8**
Focal Length:	**20.8 mm**
ISO Speed:	100
Exposure Bias:	0/100 EV
Flash:	Flash did not fire
Orientation:	Horizontal (normal)
X-Resolution:	72 dpi
Y-Resolution:	72 dpi
Software:	Adobe Photoshop CS2 Windows
Date and Time:	2007:03:01 16:44:38
YCbCr Positioning:	Co-Sited
Exposure Program:	Manual

Top photograph by Mary K. O'Connor; bottom photograph by Drew Steele.

childhood vacation spot may be able to leave out more modern details and, thus, more accurately represent the memory.

As E. H. Gombrich pointed out in his 1960 publication *Art and Illusion*, a viewer's mental set is the result of perceptual tuning in the form of selective attention, which creates a difference between looking and seeing. Considering that we cannot see without looking, we suggest that the gap between those mental sets is bridged by steps of engagement with what is being looked at. When looking at any image, the viewer is experiencing levels of engagement that we posit as a four-step process of appearance that includes attention, interest, involvement, and attitude.

Four Steps to Image Engagement (Appearance)
1. Attention   Focus
2. Interest   Cognitive awareness of the focus
3. Involvement   Meaning attached to the awareness
4. Attitude   Feeling regarding the meaning

Each of these steps often, but not always, appears to function simultaneously when objects of attention come into view, and in all cases, the time it takes to complete all of these steps makes up the structure of the engagement. To visually engage with an image, we must first focus attention on a part or parts of the image. How many parts we choose to focus on depends upon the interest-drawing capacity of the part itself (initial reason for engagement), which is a function of our own individual cognitive style, level of awareness, and experience. Once our interest is drawn to a part or parts of the image and we are aware of it, then we can, and normally do, attach some meaning to the part or parts. We might say that we generate a collection of subimage engagements and that function and meaning are directly tied to the construction and analysis of that collection. As soon as meaning is attached to the parts that have come into awareness, then some feeling (attitude) can be generated surrounding the image as a whole. Often that attitude can be as simple as "Okay, I see it, so what!"

Most of our normal waking hours are filled with an abundance of unattended images and a rash of unspoken "so whats?" In contrast, we also spend a lot of time making judgments (often only mental, sometimes verbal) about what we see. In Gombrich's terms, we could say that once a statement has been formulated, we have gone from looking to seeing. For example, "He's too fat," "She is beautiful," or "What a lovely sunset." It appears that humans have a natural tendency to have some type of attitude regarding the images they see, and attitudes can have an impact on how image structures are perceived to be different by different viewers. Movements in the art world have been both created and destroyed as a result of this fourth step in image engagement—attitude.

Dear reader, we would like you to test your own level of engagement by looking at the following photograph and then answering the questions on the next page.

Without looking back at the photograph, answer the following:

1. How much time did you spend looking at the image?
2. How many different parts did you focus on?
3. Which parts grabbed your attention?
4. How many parts do you have names for?
5. What would you call this image if it were in a collection?
6. How do you feel about this image?

We hope that this little exercise has provided some insight into the fact that there are not only image structures, structured levels of image engagement, and collection structures, but there is also structure associated with what you see, not just what is available to be seen. Our point is that viewers of images are not always interested in seeing all that is available to be seen; they usually want to see what meets their needs or accomplishes some goal and then move on, just as you did with this photo. As such, we suggest that image collections, whether public or private, should in some way be structured around those viewer objectives.

IMAGE COMPLEXITY

In order to structure image collections to conform to user and viewer objectives, the issue of image complexity bears some investigation. By image complexity, we are not necessarily referring to image size, the number of different colors, the number of pixels in a digital image, the number of shapes, the various textures depicted, provenance concerns, and other classifiable aspects of an image that are not included in the visual experience of seeing, such as identification numbers, dates, and the like. We consider image complexity as the bane of image classification because it represents the number of focal attention points (or areas) in an image that can generate meaning through cognitive awareness and result in an attitude about the image as a whole. Anyone who has viewed either the original or a copy of Leonardo da Vinci's *Mona Lisa* would be quick to say from memory that it is a portrait of a woman with an interesting smile facing the viewer's left. If asked, however, can the viewer say how many fingers are in view, whether the subject is sitting or standing, what type of flowers are on the windowsill, or if there is a roadway or a body of water pictured? Most of us would be at a loss unless we took another look and focused with interest on other parts of the painting.

The greater the number of points or areas of focal attention, the greater the potential complexity of the image. We say "potential" because every image viewer does not look at every possible focal point when viewing an image to see what is there. More importantly, as art historian James Elkins points out in his book *The Object Stares Back*, "each act of vision mingles seeing with not seeing, so that vision can become less a way of gathering information than avoiding it." Professional artists who paint, sculpt, photograph, or create other types of image artifacts for the purpose of viewing and collecting have learned to compose their works to draw focal attention to specific points or areas of the image produced. Image viewers, however, do not always abide by the creator's intent and will find meaning by directing attention to other points of interest in the image. The question then arises, should those other layers of meaning as ascribed to the image by its viewers also be terms or phrases for use in structuring a collection of images?

Since we have written this book for general audiences, we would respond that such additional layers of meaning would go a long way in helping museums and other public image collections in creating a vast array of interesting exhibitions based on viewer meanings attached to what we now know as "masterpieces" of fine art. We believe that we would quickly see traditional barriers of collection structure come tumbling down, because works could be displayed side by side based on ascribed viewer meaning instead of the art movement, period, artist, or style of composition. This is not to say that institutions have not produced such displays with professional eyes guiding the exhibit selections. We are asserting, however, that such exhibits and displays have not been assembled based on the eyes and minds of naïve viewers who have just as much right to define what they see as the professional critic, curator, or collector.

Da Vinci cannot tell us what we should see any more than we can tell him what we do see. Meaning, as such, resides in the eye's mind of the beholder, both creator and viewer, perhaps to their mutual exclusion. This circumstance occurs every time a new artist approaches a gallery with his or her portfolio of work. For example:

> Artist: "I would like you to represent me and my works. The mean-
> ing I am trying to express through these works is a sense of
> independence with a touch of humility in a world filled with
> turmoil."
> Gallery representative: "I'm sorry, I don't see it."
> Artist: "Okay, I'll take my work to another gallery."

This concept was aptly stated by Jacob Bronowski in his 1969 lecture ti-tled "The Act of Recognition," at the National Gallery of Art in Washington, D.C. To paraphrase his statement on works of art, we would say "an image is essentially an unfinished statement.... You will make your own generalization from it.... We are all individual. We all have our own inner language."

Photo by Mary K. O'Connor.

We suspect that this image can be expressed through the inner lan-guage of any viewer without it being an expression of what it is, where it is, or when it is. It is more a matter of attitude (mood or emotion) based on how the viewer focuses attention and interest in the photo.

For each of us that expression may be calming, soothing, peaceful, lonely, abandoned, or any other terms that match the photo to the cognitive state of the viewer. In a structured image collection, emotional effect is of-ten neglected for the sake of verisimilitude. Hence, we may well relinquish the right to see for the right to know. The artist, the curator, and the docent

are quick to disgorge their knowledge of an image and structure their collections in concert with that knowledge, but they seldom ask viewers what they see. The assumption has always been that until the "knowledge" has been passed on, the viewer is simply a naïve bystander staring with blind eyes.

Here is an image that is complex at the image pixel level, with numerous colors, edges, and textures strewn about the real estate of the photograph; at the clustered pixel level, with people, motorcycles, print signs, street signs, traffic light; and at a conceptual level, with helmeted police, casually dressed police, a man with a long text sign, a bookstore, a photo banner of a Nobel laureate, reflections of a golden hill, and the numerals 264. What might be going on here? Of course, we often speak of an image as if it were a window on reality and ask, "What is going on here?" when this is simply a collection of pixels with varying values resulting from some collection of elements having been in front of the camera at some time.

If you had been at this bookstore near the University of California campus in Berkeley on May 29, 2004, to catch a glimpse of Bill Clinton autographing his autobiography, you might well have seen this collection of people and things outside the door.

PHEROMONES OF MEANING

The problem with discussing meaning in association with images is that multiple definitions apply to the term. *Meaning* in the context of image engagement and complexity can stand for

1. The intended message of the image,
2. The expressed message of the image, or
3. The signified message of the image.

When structuring an image collection, it is quite difficult to include access points to each of these types of message, because often the only messages available to the image collector are the intended message based on the history and circumstances surrounding the creation of the image, or the expressed messages attached to the image as communicated by its creator and/or its critics. In almost every case, however, the number of possible *signified* messages is impossible to identify. These circumstances lead us down a different path for our discussion about structuring image collections.

In the 1950s, both E. O. Wilson in his work with ants and Adolph Butenandt in his work with silkworms discovered that these insects were able to put out powerful chemical substances that convey information and stimulate behavior responses in other like insects. In 1959, the term *pheromone* was first introduced as the common name for these chemical substances. We would propose that images act to induce humans to emit pheromones of meaning that structure the wealth of possible information that can be used for structuring and accessing them in their collections.

The best way for us to illustrate this point is to reference the original source, the insect. The pheromone scent (a chemical substance) is produced to represent an action that is required or a direction that should be taken by other insects in the same society. Traditionally, humans use words to accomplish those tasks. It is not hard to imagine writing a letter to a friend that would go something like this:

> I wanted to tell you that both Ethan and Andrew were in Texas at the same time for a few days. One of the things they decided to do was to mount an electric motor on the decked canoe I had built a few years ago—the one that used to have the hull painted green. We all thought it would be cool—actually it was over 100 degrees, so it really was hot!—if we all headed out onto the river near our house. At this time of year there is very little current, lots of particulate, and a large number of snakes in the water—perfect! We decided we should get pictures of the event, but nobody wanted to subject a good camera to the possibility of a snake attack, so we stooped and bought one of those cardboard, single-use cameras. We got the electric motor secured and working, got the other electric boat onto the water, then put in the blue Greenland-style kayak and the wooden kayak. Six miles and a few snake sightings later we all drank a lot of liquid and went out for a Thai food dinner.

We can use words to describe objects, actions, reactions, and relations. Note that in the letter above there are some first names, and there are references to different sorts of boats; there are words related to the climate of a particular state, and more than one reference to snakes. Within the illocutionary action of creating the letter, the writer had a particular purpose and knew certain things about the primary, intended audience that enabled a small collection of words to paint a picture for the intended recipients

because they know what a Greenland-style kayak looks like, because they know Ethan and Andrew, and because they have been to the river near the house. Even so, some details that might have been of interest to the intended recipients were not in the note. There is no mention of how each of the guys is wearing his hair now; there is no mention of just how the motor was attached; there was no mention of the repair job performed on the aft deck of the kayak; and the actual appearance of the clouded water is not described with any significant depth.

Within a photograph made with the cardboard, single-use camera we are presented with nearly all the detail that would have been presented to the unmediated eye at the scene—in essence, a photocutionary act that not only corresponds with the illocutionary act, but enhances it. The shape and size of each of the boats is simply evident, the motor mount arrangement is simply evident, and the look of the water with the high-angle sun on it is simply evident. The colors, textures, edges, and brightness are made evident, as if the multiple streams of light data reflected at that moment had been transected at the point of the film plane (yes, this is one case where film still holds on in the market) had been frozen in time. For the purposes of our discussion we will set aside the issues of stereopsis, the differences between RGB sensitivity in film and human eyes, the differences in resolution between the camera and the eye, and the differences in contrast ratios. However, if the original photocutionary act was to make a record of a particular set of people during a particular event, there is no ethical necessity or obligation upon the maker to represent the image for use by others. Why is this an issue? We have no way of deriving many of the ancillary bits of information from a photograph that we might be able to derive from the letter. There is nothing "Ethan" of any part of the photograph; there is nothing "Texas" inherent in the RGB; and there is nothing "electric motor" about the distribution of edges. For people familiar with previous images of Ethan, this image might evoke a similar neural response, yet there is nothing inherently Ethan in the data. There is nothing inherently "kayak," so that anybody searching a large database of images of small boats would have to know something about small boats either by experience or by previous experience with images of boats. That also means that to find an image of a kayak within a collection of hundreds or thousands of images, there would be no way to winnow the field of candidate images beforehand as one might with a verbal descriptor. The person committing the photocutionary act likely knows the objects in front of the lens and has little need to remember more than some detail for recall. That detail may or may not be sufficient for some other searcher with limited or no knowledge of the work or intentions of the original image maker to find a perfectly suitable image. We can describe images and parse collections of images with image primitives such as RGB distribution, but this is likely to be of little general utility.

As we will restate often, pictures are not words and words are not native elements of pictures (in whatever form or medium they may be), yet it remains human nature to convert pictures to words. If, however, we return to our premise that images can induce pheromones of meaning that extend beyond language for laying down a path to collection structure and access to images within that structure, then we can suggest better ways for structuring such collections.

Let us first restate the situation. To most individuals, applying word descriptors to a textual document and to an image appear to be the same sort of activity. However, they cannot be the same activity, since describing the document text is an extraction process, and there are (usually) no words to extract from an image (photo, painting, etc.). If we return to our opening definitions of *meaning* we can quickly envision the dilemma. Without words to extract, we do not know the intended message of the image, we have no expressed message, and we are left only with attempts at understanding what the image signifies. In this situation we are left only with an ability to lay down some pheromones of meaning to address these missing language elements. What might those pathways to understanding look like and would they be the same for all viewers? Probably not. However, once a path is laid down, others will be able to follow without wandering about trying to trace their own path, or others can venture out on their own and create other paths to follow. The point we are trying to make here is that without words as native elements attached to an image, the image can have multiple meanings to multiple viewers. We would argue strongly that the veracity of an image lies in the viewing engagement with the image, not in its description. So let us continue with a discussion of possible pheromones of meaning in association with boats on a hot Texas day.

First, allow us to be perfectly clear in stating that we are not arguing for the absurd. For example, we do not assume that looking at the picture of the guys in the boat would likely be construed as mountain climbing in the Arctic. However, this photo might be as applicable to New Hampshire,

Colorado, or some other country as it is to Texas, which brings us back to pheromones of meaning. If the photo reminds me of the time I went rowing a small boat on a lake in New Hampshire, then this photo engenders pheromones of meaning associated with rowboats and lakes for one viewer. It may also do the same for another viewer, and another. The path is now traced and available to others. In addition, pheromones of meaning imply emotional impact as well.

Viewing this picture of two young men in a wooden canoe brings a smile to the face of this photographer for several reasons, one of which is that they are my sons. However, our other photograph viewer who doesn't know them also has a smile on her face because she remembers how much fun she had that summer years ago with that young man on the lake in New Hampshire when looking at this photo. For another viewer of this photo, the reaction was quite different. There was a feeling of anxiety because he had an experience that resulted in being thrown out of a boat into cold rapids, and seeing this photo brought back those memories—different pheromones, a different path from the same photo that would include words like *fear*, *dread*, and *unnerved* and would take the place of words like *enjoyment*, *love*, *excitement*, and *fun*.

This point brings us to community collections such as Flickr and their uses. These collections are not maintained to provide any particular sort of access for any particular users or uses. The large photocutionary act of such collections is the simple provision of a storage place.

Trinity River 103 degrees

Thumbnails   Detail   Comments

View as slideshow
(New window)

click here to add a description

22 photos | 44 views | Add a comment?

Photos are from 16 Jul 06.

The space also comes with tools that enable the use of illocutionary acts, such as finding images by the same photographer or using words linked to the images to find the images. However, there is no constraint on any photographer using the collection space to commit an illocutionary act that will establish a pheromone trail. Many images on Flickr are labeled simply with a camera-supplied file number, perhaps even less useful for parsing a collection than an acquisition number in a library or museum collection, which might at least provide relative dating information. A photographer may well be aware that it is easy to forget exactly where or when a particular image was made and, so, commit the illocutionary act of laying down a scent known only to the photographer. As we write this sentence, there are 5,192,833 images that are tagged with "me" in the Flickr collection. At the same time there are 135,463 pictures tagged "kayak." Two examples point to a significant difficulty. At this time there is a Flickr site with 1,001 images in the collection, of which 65 are tagged "kayak," while inspection shows 101 images that have a whole kayak or a significant portion of a kayak in the image. Inspection of all 775 images labeled "kayak" in another Flickr collection yielded 148 images that had no visible portion of a kayak but were taken while on a kayak trip and included images of roasting marshmallows, birds, children, sunsets, and other people and objects.

In an environment such as Flickr, the ability to mark images as favorites, the ability to establish sets of people whose images one wants to check on a regular basis ("contacts"), and the use of tags all present quasi-established pheromone trails. A searcher is not left to stumble blindly onto desired or usable images. If I know I generally like the images of photographer X, I can check my contacts regularly or even receive an announcement of the posting of a new image. Similarly, if I know I like the work of photographer X and I am looking for something that I know does not exist in the collection put together by X, it is fairly reasonable to check the images that X has marked as favorites. Along the same line of thinking, I might search for tags within the collection of X or within the collections of X's favorites and contacts. This *elementary category theory* (if the images made by X are within the class of photographs I regard highly, then photos regarded highly by X are likely to be in the class of photos I regard highly) does not provide an ironclad guarantee that I will find useful images by following these trails, but it presents a higher probability of success than dumb luck.

The illocutionary act of the photographer who decides to label an image with a label that is likely to make the image available to others who might be searching for images likely to be described by that word or set of words is a photocutionary act. It is an act intended to make the image available. It may also be seen as a purposeful laying down of a pheromone of meaning. This does not mean that all people searching for an image of some particular object or concept represented by the illocutionary act will necessarily find the particular image, since they may use other words at different levels of generality or words in a different language or words that are synonyms. Likewise, the decision by the photographer or by some viewer of a particular image to add an image to a group or to mark that image as a favorite is a photocutionary act, for it purposefully sets the image out for others besides the photographer. If viewer A likes a photograph made by photographer P and adds it as a "favorite," then there is some reasonable chance that people who like the images and favorites of A will find their way to the work of P in another version of the pheromones of meaning.

As we close this chapter on image engagement and complexity, we advocate that images are like people in the sense that we tend to be attracted to some and tend to avoid others. In order to accomplish that, most image viewers create verbal pathways both to and from images in order to serve their visual needs.

CHAPTER SEVEN

IMAGE USE

An element in the situation that must never be left out of account: the function an image is expected to serve.

E. H. Gombrich

FUNCTION, PURPOSE, USE

With his comment on the importance of the "function an image is expected to serve," Gombrich at once focuses our attention and opens several avenues of discussion. Earlier we discussed photocutionary acts as the purposeful construction of photographs and the purposeful use of photographs. We suggested that, while the making of the photograph may be a unitary action with a single intended function, people other than the original photographer or even the original photographer at a different time might make a purposeful use of some photograph, and that use might or might not have some relation to the original intended function. Our premise is that every image that strikes a human eye has the potential for being useful. There may be some limiting cases. A photographer may make an image and decide that it does not meet some standard for serving its intended function—poor exposure, poor composition—and so destroy the image. Here the utility of the image may be said to have been to give the photographer an evaluative opportunity. Perhaps the image would have served some other purpose for some other viewer perfectly well, but its failure to meet some standard of utility removes it from the pool of subsequent uses. Another limiting case could be the image that does not meet the needs of some original intent, survives for subsequent viewing, and demonstrates that the well-known photographic artist was capable of less than exemplary work. Then we might consider the photocutionary act of going back to old collections, whether a box of discarded snapshots or the photo morgue of a defunct publication. Even when the original intent cannot be discerned, a subsequent viewer may be able to make some use of the data. The nature of the utility of any particular image, however, is not always easily defined, because just as image meaning may be different to different constituencies, so too is image use. We might recast some aspects of the photocutionary acts model in terms of three words:

Function: A thing (an image) that depends on and varies in relation to
               something else
  Purpose: The reason for which something (an image) exists
      Use: The action or service into which something (an image) is put

Although the conceptual and definitional boundaries are not necessarily distinct, we can achieve some level of pragmatic clarity by suggesting that image use may be defined differently by an image creator, an image collector, and an image viewer. We view image function, purpose, and use in the following manner:

Image creator: Considers *purpose* as the primary instrument for creating
                  the image, is not always sure that it will function in that
                  manner, and often does not know how it will be used. For
                  example:
                     1. Purpose: To make a political statement
                     2. Function: Means by which the image purpose is
                        understood
                     3. Use: Hopefully, exposure to public view
Image collector: Considers *function* as the primary component for seeking
                  out images with a purpose that is clearly defined, and
                  where use is subordinated to purpose. For example:
                     1. Function: Politicized imagery for public display
                     2. Purpose: To educate a viewing audience
                     3. Use: Attraction of interested viewers
Image viewer: Considers *use* as the primary driver for looking at images,
                  with levels of interest in purpose that range from casual
                  to intense, and mostly negligible concern for function.
                     1. Use: Desire for increased knowledge about the
                        image(s)
                     2. Purpose: Curiosity ranging to professional
                        requirement
                     3. Function: May or may not care how the image functions, depending on 2 (purpose)

We hope that the above has stimulated the reader's thinking about how different interests can influence image viewing and the nature of human engagement with images. Using one more example, we believe our viewpoint will become clearer:

Image subject matter: Advertisements
Images: Cigarette packages with printed advertising
  Image creator: 1 Concern = Purpose: Influence the buying public

                    2 Concern = Function: Sell cigarettes
                    3 Concern = Use: To be viewed by the public at large
Image collector: 1 Concern = Function: Examples of cigarette advertising
                    2 Concern = Purpose: Assemble a history of the industry
                    3 Concern = Use: Various (book, film, album, etc.)
  Image viewer: 1 Concern = Use: Look at or don't look at (packages or ads)
                    2 Concern = Purpose: Should I or should I not consider
                              smoking
                    3 Concern = Function: The Marlboro Man looks really
                              cool! Or, I think I'll heed the warning label.

Before moving ahead and describing a list of various image uses that can influence the nature of viewing and the structures of image collections, glance at the photographs below from three points of view: (1) As just a casual observer of the images, (2) as someone who might want these images in their collection of images, and (3) as someone who intentionally created these images. Are your viewpoints the same in each case?

These are photos of one of the authors and his younger brother. The time span between photos is fifty years. Let's first look at these images from the creator's point of view stemming from *purpose*, that is, why these photos were taken. First, we must take account of the word *creator* as it is used here. The image of the boys was created by their mother. She had the idea for the picture and she brought out the camera, she got the boys onto the steps, and she actually pushed the shutter release on the camera. The image of the men sitting on the same steps was, in a sense, a joint creation; the

idea of a photo of the two people some fifty years later was David's (the younger brother), the idea of the re-creation of the step photo was Brian's (the older brother), and the shutter release was pressed by their father. Such joint authorship or creation is not at all unusual in amateur or professional photography.

As to the purpose of each of the photographs, we can say there were multiple linked purposes within each of the photocutionary events and across the two events. The woman who made the image of the boys was an accomplished amateur painter and craftsperson who had access to what would now be termed a prosumer 35mm camera. She wanted a memory of her boys, she wanted to be able to share their appearances with her mother living in another state, and she wanted a nice springtime picture. When her sons decided to replicate the image it was to accomplish a "cool" photocutionary act, it was to have the opportunity to look at and discuss the original image with their mother, it was to engage their father in this photo memory act, and it was to honor their parents for the love and good times represented by that porch. Note that in the second image there is the face of an older woman on the porch. This is the mother who shot the original image. While she did not want to be prominent in a photograph, she did agree to be in it as a "memory."

How did the creator of these images intend them to *function*? The photograph of the young boys would have functioned as part of a package of images that would have come in the mail from the photo processor. The package would have been opened with some anticipation around the dinner table and each image looked at and commented on in turn. Later, all the images, except any blanks or terribly out of focus photos, would have been mounted in a photo album that would be brought out and looked at when company came by or when some rainy day dictated indoor activity. The negative of the image of the boys on the porch steps would have been sent to the photo processor with a request for a duplicate print. Upon the arrival of the duplicate in the mail, it would have been checked and then wrapped inside the sheets of paper on which a letter to Grandma had been written by the boys and their mother. The grandmother had a small box in which she kept photographs.

The image from fifty years later has functioned rather differently. It was born digital, so there was no wait of several days for processing, and there was rather little ceremony involved in everyone looking at the LCD panel on the back of the camera. The image was printed on an ink-jet printer a little later in the day, with copies made for everyone involved. A little later, both images were uploaded to Flickr so that they would be available to anybody at any time. While the earlier image functioned as two physical copies, the later image exists in several formats and is available for manipulation and presentation in other forms.

And, with purpose and function in mind, how did the creator of these images intend to put them to *use*?

Use 1: The creator of the first image basically wanted a memory piece. It was a technically well-made memory.

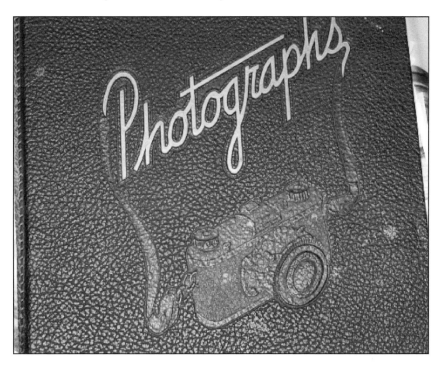

Use 2: The actual making provided a form of secondary use, that of practic-
ing photographic skills. Making a copy of the photograph to send to
Grandma was a sharing and bonding use of the image, though it too was
based on the primary memory use.

Use 3: Now it must be said that there was a use made by a secondary user,
the older son. A modified version of the image appeared as an illustration
within an essay on the memory function of photographs. There was never
any thought of publication in the mind of the mother who made the
image, though she was happy to see it put to such a use. Of course, the
same is to be said about the use of that image on these pages.

Now let's consider the image collector whose first concern is generally
function. What function could these images serve?

Function 1: Demonstrate examples of change

   a. How people change
   b. How clothes change
   c. How construction materials change
   d. How photographic processes have changed
   e. The results of aging

Function 2: Demonstrate the concept of "taking different directions"

   a. Looking in different directions
   b. One brother a university professor, the other a professional bounty
      hunter
   c. Vertical and horizontal lattice work in one photo, but diagonal in the
      other

Function 3: Demonstrate concerns for safety over time

   a. Railings on the steps that were missing in the earlier photo
   b. Height of the stair risers more conducive for safe ascension
   c. Enclosed versus open wood railing on porch

Lastly, let's consider the image viewer who, as most readers of this book,
would be interested in how these images could be used (other than to reinforce our commentary).

Use 1: To show how fifty years can change a person, or not
Use 2: As an example of how the T-shirt is still a major fashion item
Use 3: Changing times and circumstances, but families tending to stay together

Why have we gone to such great lengths to emphasize these distinctions between purpose, function, and use? The answer lies in the comment
made by E. H. Gombrich in his 1999 publication of *The Uses of Images*: "If

we are no longer allowed to speak in terms of means and ends, all images embody the intention of their creators."

Our discourse on *purpose*, *function*, and *use* is intended to point out that an image collection can be structured around any or all of these manifestations of visual engagement with an image. Often, however, a single individual is required by choice or profession to become involved with images by taking on only one of these roles, so it is important to note how the role can influence how the image is being considered, and how the means and ends associated with that image can change.

USING AND ABUSING IMAGES

The subject of image use has been the focus of numerous publications and, just as important, across a variety of academic disciplines. We have gleaned a list that, although not complete, is comprehensive enough to identify how both image structure and image collection structures can be enhanced or confounded by these various uses:

- Reinforce memory (family photos)
- Create a record of the past (museum collections)
- Promote doctrine (religious icons)
- Rouse interest (tattoos)
- Instruct (textbook illustrations)
- Influence (advertisements)
- Coerce (traffic signs)
- Temper the spirit (flags)
- Invoke ownership (graffiti)
- Incite to act (political imagery)
- Put up a defense (protest signs)
- Support a cause or enterprise (logos)
- Engender value (sports cards, Beanie Babies, and the like)
- Act as a gateway to understanding (all of the above)

It should be apparent from this line of thinking that *use* is part and parcel of a cognitive conglomerate that includes both function and purpose. The significant difference is the human visual experience that intercedes between the image and its meaning and invokes some form of understanding. As John Gilmour, professor of philosophy, states in *Picturing the World*, visual culture is not a language. The visual world depends on meanings and practices shared with other people. We emphasize here that image collections are an integral part of the visual world, and practices surrounding their development and structure depend on shared practice and understanding. It might seem that image creators, collectors, and viewers should be put on an equal footing to have a strong foundation to support an image collection. However, the complexity of the possible relationships, the variety of funding and administrative arrangements behind image collections (from the shoebox to the Getty), and the sheer number of photographs in the world constrain the possibilities of such equal footing. For example, the following anecdote about one image that, on the face of it, illustrates how tattoos "rouse interest" actually speaks to a variety of possible relationships and levels of understanding. We offer the following as a sample engagement with a photograph.

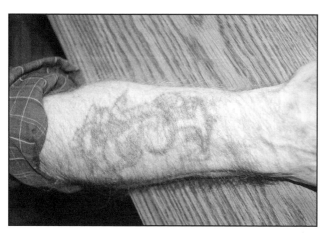

Tattoos and those tattooed.

In 1944, a young sailor went, "half-cocked," to a tattoo artist whom he realized was half-cocked too! He asked for this design—basically an eagle, the letters USN, and a ship's anchor. "Son of a bitch, this is going to hurt, but I'm going to do it anyway." For years after the war, people would come up and ask, "Were you in the Navy? Where did you serve?" Now, as he said recently, fewer and fewer people ask, probably fewer and fewer even know the meaning.

So, the tattoo itself was an image. It was made with the use of an outline pattern, so there were hundreds or thousands of men wearing a version of that picture on their arms. The meaning and the collection were dependent on those seeing the images. For two or three decades after World War II, the collection was just as much a collection of sailors as it was a collection of eagle and anchor pictures. The collection of people who would know the military significance has dwindled, as has the number of men still alive who had gotten the tattoo, so the image collection has changed. Now, old men with a few almost indistinguishable blue lines on their arms constitute the image group. Since the best inks for tattoos at that time came from Japan, and since Japan was not a good source during the war, the color that originally made the tattoos on sailors' arms so striking has all but disappeared. Even if most or all of the men were still alive today, the collection of images would have changed.

Our whole existence from a visual perspective is for the purpose of survival. And as we look to old brain functions, the initial purpose of visual introspection was for "fight or flight" reactions. As we look at the human visual system some thousands of years later, we find human dealings with images as a continuation of that original function. As such, we can further expand our list of image uses to include:

Episodic narrative: As seen often in various forms that include, but are certainly not limited to, mosaics, stained glass, frescoes, murals, and tapestries depicting heroic feats.

Body decoration:	To keep evil spirits at bay or to gain strength against the unknown, such as amulets, which have given way to jewelry and other adornments.
Identification:	Costumes, uniforms, insignias, and the more advanced images that include fingerprints, iris scans, and traffic camera photos and videos.
Focus of devotion:	Idols, religious icons, and the like.
Guardians against intrusion:	Gargoyles and similar architectural elements.
Syncretistic beliefs:	Merging of pagan belief with religious doctrine such as the Celtic cross.

With an ever-increasing abundance of images over time, the expanded use of images has contributed to an even more interesting array of possible purposes.

Seduce:	Images that appeal by enhancing, embellishing, and overstating, for example, Joe Camel.
Corrupt:	Images that promote or entice a person to act in a way that may not be in their best interests; for example, images that make gambling look like fun.
Create trends:	Fashion images would be a good example.
Provide aesthetic enjoyment:	Any image, considering that beauty is in the eye of the beholder.
Attract attention:	Signs, posters, billboards, and the like.
Build ego:	Badges, medals, trophies, decals, and ribbons.
Confirm prejudice:	Symbols designed to promote exclusivity, expel inclusiveness, and foster xenophobia.
Unite or hold together:	Totems, emblems, flags, and like images.
Reduce anxiety:	Considered to be unique to an individual viewer, but often includes views of water, sky, or flowers.
Characterize:	Portraits that embrace actual features, as well as cartoons or caricatures that focus on those features disproportionately.
Memorialize:	Through use of an effigy.
Ridicule:	One of the most prominent examples would be the political cartoon.

Let us also note that in the modern era, as in times past, we often denote progress with imagery that is used to

Deviate from convention:	Any creative works that do not fit into what are considered to be the acceptable norms and visual genres of the time, such as new schools of art and new art forms.

Summing up (but not concluding) our comments on use, we take one step backward by confirming that throughout history another major use of images has been to consciously or unwittingly

Perpetuate   Depictions of believed truths in the absence of substantiated
ignorance: knowledge. Prime examples could include early maps,
              conceptualizations of the solar system, images of religious value
              and significance based on unsubstantiated doctrine, and Albrecht
              Durer's 1515 incorrect drawing of a rhinoceros that appeared in
              natural history books up until the nineteenth century.

LOOKING AT OR LOOKING FOR

In this continuing discussion about image use, it is important to note that image viewers approach visual engagement from two perspectives that can have considerable impact on how a collection is structured. The first perspective includes the concept of "looking at" an image. This includes having chance encounters, making initial observations, scanning the environment, directing attention to specific objects in the visual field, and being directed by others to look at specific images you may or may not have seen before. The function of looking at objects is solely for the purpose of identification: What am I seeing?

     Most collections, both public and private, tend to be structured around the *looking at* experience. What this means is that the placement of the visual objects in the collection often includes both descriptive and explanatory information so that the viewer will be able to answer the primary question: "What am I seeing?" While this functional objective is professionally accepted as the norm for maintaining and perpetuating an interesting collection of image objects (paintings, sculptures, period pieces, historic artifacts, contemporary creations, and other collectibles), it may fall short of providing image viewers with what they may require in terms of a second perceptual objective, one that encompasses the "looking for" concept.

Looking for an image object within a collection entails a whole other set of behaviors that are supplemental to the "looking at" activities. We would argue that most collection oversight activities give short shrift to this important aspect of image viewing. In other words, the brief descriptors that act as collection dividing categories are most often expected to fulfill those viewing needs; that is, in the public domain, if we're looking for a visually pleasing landscape painting, we probably cannot go to the Landscape Paintings Gallery. Instead, we will be given the opportunity to go to several galleries located on several floors, each of which may be variously called European Paintings, Asian Art, American Art, Contemporary Art, or Prints, Drawings and Photographs. Or, in the absence of those broad categories of collection structure, we might be faced with designations such as Dutch, Flemish, Italian, French, and so forth, or, Fifteenth Century, Sixteenth Century, and so on.

Just so the reader does not misconstrue our intention with the above commentary, we would further clarify that many institutions have made great strides in addressing the "looking for" nature of viewer engagements with their respective collections by representing their collections or portions thereof in online environments where viewers can search for their exact needs. However, based on current technologies and the authority invested in the designers of the online collection, many of these resources still fall short

of meeting the needs of an online viewer of the collection images. Often the required image may reside in the collection; however, it still eludes viewing because access to it has been restricted to the terminology associated with the physical entity in the collection. In other words, the viewer can conduct an online search based on a specific need; however, the search terms (keywords) used for that search must coincide with the words used to describe and/or explain that image as used in the physical collection itself, which leads us to our concluding comments on image use.

So, *looking for* an image entails greater cognitive effort on the part of the searcher than merely *looking at* an image. Looking for an image can include a variety of other intended uses that extend beyond the image uses ascribed to creators of images and collectors of images. The image viewer may have other requirements that could possibly include the following additional uses:

Disorder or disarray: Images characterizing an abnormal state or situation.

Distillation: Images that demonstrate a separation of common elements.

Isolation: An adjunct to distillation, but related more to a sense of emotional or physical separation.

Simplification: Images that leave out elements that distract from the focal point(s) of the image.

Thematization: Images that subordinate to a topic without specifically representing it.

Distortion: Images that depict some type of optical interference.

Subversion: Images that corrupt the normal view of something, but not involving distortion.

Amplification: Images that increase the strength of visual focus.

Deception: Images that are misleading, for example, certain works of the artist M. C. Escher.

Devotion: Images that instill a willingness to love or serve.

Self-expression: The most unique of image uses, that is: "Show me an image, not including a photo or painting of yourself, that best portrays who you are."

Ideally, as technologies for producing images continue to burgeon, the methods for collecting, storing, and accessing those images will also keep pace. Given our discussions above, we suggest that it is difficult to say just what "keeping pace" might mean. We can suggest that, as more and more images are made and image collections are built, a variety of access points that enable viewers of those collections to look at and to look for images is warranted. We also note that Internet-based entities such as Flickr and other like entities bring the wisdom of many individuals and their individual means of using and functioning to the problems of access.

EXHIBITIONS, ALBUMS, AND SHARE CROPPING

History portends the future, and as such we direct the reader to Giovanni Paolo Panini's painting of the *Picture Gallery of Cardinal Silvio Valenti Gonzaga* (1740), housed in the Wadsworth Atheneum Museum of Art, in Hartford, Connecticut (www.wadsworthatheneum.org). The painting provides clear evidence of the human condition when it comes to image collections and their structure. Images with all of their functions, purposes, and uses generally maintain as their least common denominators (1) instruments of knowledge, and (2) instruments of possession. In Panini's painting we see a floor-to-ceiling, wall-to-wall collection of paintings belonging to (possessed by) Cardinal Gonzaga for the edification (knowledge enhancement) of the cardinal and other viewers of the collection. Almost three hundred years later, we find ourselves doing those same things with our various image collections.

When is a collection not simply a collection? When it's an exhibition. An exhibition is simply a public presentation; however, it bears mention in this discussion of image use. One of the most common is the museum exhibition. The reasons that an exhibition falls outside of our earlier definition of collection are the following:

1. An exhibition is usually a representation of parts of the whole (collection), though, of course, it need not be.
2. An exhibition usually presents a different agenda from the purpose of the collection(s) from which it is drawing items.
3. An exhibition is often structured differently than a whole collection of similar items.
4. An exhibition, by its very nature, is temporary, not permanent.

When it comes to image use, however, the exhibition becomes a vital adjunct to whole collections because the "whole" collection is often a function of varied and diverse locations and ownerships. The exhibition can create a coming together of those separated items and present them to the public in a specific context. On the surface, public viewing of museum exhibitions may appear to be a good thing, although David Dean, in his book *Museum Exhibition: Theory and Practice*, notes that "While profit may not be the specific motive, museums have the desire to "sell" the institution, change attitudes, modify behavior, and increase conformity (of knowledge). If we follow this line of thinking, we could include each of these motives as purposes, functions, and uses of images as they play their distinct roles in accomplishing any and all of the above as part of an institutional exhibition.

We would also like to add that *albums*, like exhibitions, often present a condensed view of a whole collection. The most common are personal or family photo albums that usually contain the most liked or most representative examples of the people or situations that a person wants to put on view or have instantaneously available for reference or recollection. The album of-

ten differs from the collection as a whole because it generally has no explanatory notes, dates may or may not be included, and many times viewers of such albums require descriptions, explanations, and interpretations to be supplied by the owner(s) of the album.

However, with the advent of online photographic services, the nature of the family photo album has taken on a new dimension where titles, descriptions, and detailed explanations can be included and made available to others instanta-neously without the album being relegated to its normal coffee table loca-tion. So the personal album, which was a private collection within a collection (many people did not include duplicate or technically poor images), becomes public on Flickr and thus is an exhibition within a massive collection.

Image utility is expansive. We have touched on but a few of the possible uses to which an image can be put. In closing this chapter, we would also like to note that the varieties of image editing programs, techniques, and serv-ices have also increased along with the proliferation of available, collected, and stored images. Now both professional and novice have the capability of taking almost any image that can be printed or photographed, scanning it, cropping it, coloring it, and creating dozens of effects that make multiple iter-ations of the single image for a variety of possible uses. And, as heard in a recent television advertisement: "Just think, I can assemble my whole collec-tion of vacation photos and send them to everyone in my family ... and no one can stop me!" It has long been said that a picture is worth a thousand words; modern technologies have now given us the opportunity to make a picture worth a thousand other pictures.

PART III

IMAGE COLLECTIONS

A collection is a mistress of another kind, safer and more exciting. . . .
Hans Kraus (noted book and manuscript dealer)

The concept of image collecting dates back over 30,000 years to collections of images painted on cave walls. Without delving deeply into the underlying psychology, it appears that something about human nature drives us to collect things. Werner Muensterberger, a retired associate professor of psychiatry, in his work *Collecting: An Unruly Passion*, believes that all efforts to collect are compensatory. In other words, collecting things takes the place of something we don't have or can't have, and collectors, for the most part, have an unrelenting need for acquisition. Romans collected Greek works out of envy. History further points to relics such as skulls and bones as prime collectibles due to their presumed power to preserve and perpetuate life. While relics were able to bridge the gap between pagan practices and Christian beliefs, religious art served to educate the illiterate and thus became a source of prime collectibles all the way up to the fifteenth century. Then, from the mid-1400s to the mid-1500s, a shift began to appear in paintings, from religious to more secular themes. Collectors were also exposed to more items of visual curiosity as new trade routes were opened.

Two names stand out for the purpose of this discussion: Jean de Berry (1340–1416) and Emperor Rudolph II (1552–1612). Jean de Berry was considered the medieval world's best-known collector and connoisseur of the visual arts, and Emperor Rudolph II was described at the time as the greatest art patron in the world. These collections represent the early beginnings of what today we would call structured collections, involving methods of classification and the orderly categorization of the objects they contained. Shortly after Emperor Rudolph's death, an impressive volume representing only part of his holdings was published, with 125 etchings and descriptions of the objects in his vast collection. In retrospect, we could consider that to be one of the earliest catalogues of a structured collection of images. Although these collections do not predate efforts of the Catholic Church to start a library around the fourth century, they do relate to the Vatican's interest in collected artworks, which took place during the pontificate of Julius II. Pope Julius II was a great patron of Renaissance art, and in 1505, he took up the task begun by Pope Nicholas V to expand construction of St. Peter's, which involved the commissioned works of Raphael and Michelangelo.

While painted, etched, and sculpted works, along with cultural artifacts, have been at the forefront of collectible genres for hundreds of years, the advent of photography and cinematography changed the landscape of collectible images at the beginning of the twentieth century. At the beginning of the twenty-first century that landscape is changing even more.

Tow truck with museum sign.

CHAPTER EIGHT

WHAT'S IN A WORD?

No one has ever said that there must be a verbalization in correspondence with every phase of understanding.

Umberto Eco

ONE WAY OF thinking about representing individual image documents within a collection is to compare the individual piece against the entire list of descriptors and determine if each of the descriptors does or does not work for that image. Imagine that we have 100,000 words total describing items in our collection. For each new item we could ask if descriptor one works; if descriptor two works; if descriptor three works; all the way up to descriptor 100,000. Obviously, most pairs of items and descriptors will have negative responses checked off, but many will not. Then, for retrieval, a person seeking an image could go through the entire vocabulary and check off those terms that might describe images that would be useful. The retrieval system would then look for matches between item descriptor lists and retrieval request descriptor lists. Ordinarily, we use heuristics to avoid the time-consuming effort involved, but the basic construct can be instructive for our thoughts on how we might describe an item. Most descriptive systems use words to describe picture objects in an image, though this is not necessarily the only approach.

If we define language as a higher order cognitive process that allows us to communicate with each other with purpose, then words used as labels for things can be considered tools for establishing purposeful communications. Likewise, creating a structured collection of images based on words requires an underlying framework that connects the collection to its viewers through purposeful communications. A difficulty arises, however, when purposeful communication based on words is associated with a perceptual paradigm based on prior assumptions. By prior assumptions, we mean prior *assertions*. For example, what should a structured collection of images look like in terms of the words associated with the images contained in those collections? The normal approach or tendency of professionals that oversee institutional collections, of business enterprises interested in managing their digital assets, and of private collectors that organize their unique collectables is to use existing paradigms based on words and word groupings to provide access points to images in their collections.

The basic problem inherent in this type of approach is that words not only are labels for objects, they also are labels for features, attributes, and characteristics of objects as mentally assessed and assigned by viewers of those image objects. On the basis of such conditions, we could create a table of linguistic values that would describe images in a collection, as follows.

Image object		
Label 1: L1	Yes	No
Label 2: L2	Yes	No
Label 3: L3	Yes	No
Label 4: L4	Yes	No
Label 5: L5	Yes	No
Label N: Ln	Yes	No
Image has this feature		
Feature 1: F1	Yes	No
Feature 2: F2	Yes	No
Feature 3: F3	Yes	No
Feature 4: F4	Yes	No
Feature 5: F5	Yes	No
Feature N: Fn	Yes	No
Image has this characteristic		
Characteristic 1: C1	Yes	No
Characteristic 2: C2	Yes	No
Characteristic 3: C3	Yes	No
Characteristic 4: C4	Yes	No
Characteristic 5: C5	Yes	No
Characteristic N: Cn	Yes	No
Image has this attribute		
Attribute 1: A1	Yes	No
Attribute 2: A2	Yes	No
Attribute 3: A3	Yes	No
Attribute 4: A4	Yes	No
Attribute 5: A5	Yes	No
Attribute N: An	Yes	No

(Yes = acceptable description; No = not an acceptable description)

Considering that this approach to image description and collection structure may cause some confusion, let us clarify the argument with some definitions.

Label: Can refer to a title; however, that discriminates against the viewer by placing authority in the hands of the image

creator and discounts what the viewer sees. Image labels
can also be used to describe the genre of the image.

Feature: A word that describes what stands out in the image as a
prominent quality from a viewer's point of view.

Characteristic: A word that describes a differentiating quality of the image
that makes it different or the same as other images within
a collection of images.

Attribute: A word that relates to the image that may or may not
actually be present in the visual field.

To demonstrate the logic associated with these concepts of linguistic
value attributable to an image, let's look at the following images.

**Random images from the National Oceanic and Atmospheric Administration database of
photographs (www.noaa.gov).**

In one of our earlier investigations, twenty-eight viewers were asked to
describe these images with words that could act as points of access if the
images were part of a larger collection. Keep in mind that the images presented to the viewers were in gray scale similar to these. The following are
some of the results of that inquiry.

Green	Blue
Boat	Fishing
Happy	Beautiful

The question we pose is "Are those descriptions wrong?" The answer
we pose is "No." If an image is capable of possessing labels, features, characteristics, and attributes that engender words for possible description, then
any of those words could possibly be used to facilitate access to such images
in a database of images. In the examples above, none of the six descriptive
words is physically present in the image, yet viewers considered those words
as appropriate descriptors.

Without belaboring the issue, we suggest that access to images in a collection not only involves their arrangement in physical space, but also necessarily involves their arrangement in cognitive space. Hence, image accessibility in a collection of images is simply a function of the extent to which an image is made inaccessible. Images cannot just be labeled. We have entered an age in which functional access to digitized images has become a major concern, especially in the realm of information retrieval. The efficacy surrounding retrieval system development remains mired in issues of constant overlap, inconsistent membership among and between images, and the insistence that traditional methods of cataloguing and indexing can save the day. One of the greatest difficulties, yet to be overcome, is the often adumbrative, impressionistic, and abstract nature of viewers' cognitive engagements with images.

USING LANGUAGE TO STRUCTURE AN IMAGE COLLECTION

In chapter 5 we introduced some of the difficulties associated with the assignment of words to describe images. However, a variety of organizing tools for structuring image collections involve assigning words to images in order to facilitate their acquisition, accommodate their storage, make them accessible, and stimulate viewing pleasure. These tools, however, have been used mainly in the realm of large public collections. Word-based description of image documents points to another issue surrounding the structure of image collections. Who are the intended viewers of the collection? From such a perspective, we posit that there are four broad categories of structured image collections.

Public collection:	Contains images that are available to the public at large. For example, any institution (library, museum, gallery, public building, or online image posting site) where the image objects are available at no charge to the viewing public.
Semipublic collection:	Contains images that are available to a select population of viewers as determined by the authority that oversees the collection. For example, any institution, organization, or private entity that requires a fee or membership for viewing the image objects in the collection.
Semiprivate collection:	Contains images that are available only to a set of viewers specifically selected directly by the owner(s) of the collection. For example, private collections open to select populations for viewing or online image posting sites with sharing opportunities.
Private collection:	Contains image objects viewable only by the owner of the collection. For example, any collection where the owner does

not want anyone else to know about its contents for a variety of reasons, including its value, security, and/or legal consequences.

The ability to use words to describe images in each of these types of collection poses different sets of issues. Let us begin this discussion by returning to the photo of "Andrew and Mary," referred to in chapter 5 and pictured again below.

TYPES OF COLLECTION DESCRIPTIONS

We begin by asking: Which overarching set of words is needed to make this image accessible and understandable to the audience for which it is intended, as defined by one of the types of collections noted above? By "set of words" we mean the type of word groupings that best access, describe, and explain the content of the collection to the viewing audience. Although extensive overlap exists in the following types of word groups, each set can act as a framework or supporting structure for an image collection, and its use most likely will depend on the size of the collection, the diversity of the collection, and the type of viewing audience for whom the collection is intended.

Lists

Whether public or private, most image collections involve lists. A list is simply text that is categorized, and often the categories are entered into the list in ascending alphabetic or numeric order. A list is the least common denominator when it comes to creating word categories to organize a group of things. In this case, the things are images. In our list of image things, the image above could simply be listed as "photos" or photographs. Oftentimes, lists can be used as labels to identify the location of images that are not in view, such as the contents of a box or the contents of a storeroom.

Indexes

An index is a set of pointers to the content within a specific set of data. Recognizing that our list of things contains a specific set of data called photos, we next decide whether our collection will include many different categories of photos. If so, we should create an index that includes the types of photos on our list that we would like to categorize within subheadings (another list).

Using our example image, and thinking about other photos in the collection, we might create an index category under the photos subhead called "O'Connor family." And, thus, our problems with using words for images begin. If we want to create easy access to this photo for the greatest number of viewers (including the owner of the collection), are the words *O'Connor* and *family* the best ones to use? Of necessity, we are almost forced to cognitively consider the full extent of what this photo collection includes in its entirety now and may include in the future, which could suggest indexing categories such as Acting silly, Andrew, College, Body building, 2000?, Sons, Humboldt State University, Andrew's dorm room, and Andrew and Mary. Is this a one-of-a-kind photo or are there (will there be) others that would be similar enough to this photo that they should all be in the same category that may not be called "O'Connor family"? Stop and consider for the moment that, so far, we are only talking about one photo in what we hope will be a well-structured collection.

Directories

If we quickly recognize that the extent of this collection, both now and in the future, will contain hundreds (possibly thousands) of images, it is important to consider where these images will reside. Whether in boxes in the attic (a museum storeroom or warehouse), in photo albums (in picture frames on the wall or in display cabinets), or in an online database (public or private), some type of directory will probably be needed for telling the owners and viewers of the collection where these images are located.

A directory is a list that is arranged based on sets of topics and subtopics that facilitate access to the location of the object (image) being

sought. A directory entry can be as simple as Box 2/O'Connor Family/
Andrew or as complicated as North Pavilion/Sixteenth Century/Italian/Por-
traits/Pope Clement VII. It is not a coincidence that computerized files are
also organized in directories. One of the authors has the O'Connor image
shown above in the following directory on his computer:

C:\\Documents and Settings\Howard\Desktop\BookMisc\Manuscript.

Most private and semiprivate image collections, and most small to
medium-size image collections (the reader can judge relative size based on
an understanding of their own needs), do not require a structure that goes
beyond a *list* of contents, an *index* to identify the content categories and sub-
categories, and a *directory* to assist in accessing image location. The next
types of word groups have been used mainly for public and semipublic
image collections but are not restricted to them.

Catalogues

Cataloguing is the systematic organization of information or materials so that
they can be retrieved when requested. A catalogue record will usually be
based on some formatting and content rules for the information about some
retrievable item such as a book, a picture, or physical object. Experience has
shown that the use of bibliographic cataloguing rules, when imposed on the
creation of catalogues associated with image collections, often fall short of
the robustness needed to produce functional retrievability. However, not all
catalogues are designed for the purpose of retrieval.

Most public and semipublic institutions that provide access to image
collections offer their viewing audiences some type of catalogue that acts as
an advertisement to the public by describing the nature of their holdings.
This type of catalogue is a descriptive list of items that are owned by a specific entity and can be in the form of a printed book, pamphlet, or brochure
or included (possibly in a different form) on an institution's Web site. Be
assured at this juncture that author O'Connor does not have a printed catalogue of the O'Connor Family photo collection. However, Web sites, such
as that of the Uffizi Gallery in Florence, Italy (www.virtualuffizi.com
/uffizi/index.htm), will provide you with a complete catalogue of the works in
their collection. In fact, the Uffizi Web page title says: Virtual Uffizi Florence: The Complete Catalogue.

The following additional tools (ways to group words) for structuring
image collections are the ones most focused on in the professional literature
and the least understood by the general image-viewing public.

Thesauri

A thesaurus is a standardized list used to control entry points to a collection.
This means that anyone using a thesaurus designed to access images within

a collection must choose the predefined words to find images in that collection. Most important to this discussion, however, is that the preconstructed controlling vocabulary is assumed by its creators to be complete.

For example, the *Art and Architecture Thesaurus* (AAT) contains approximately 125,000 terms and other information about artistic and architectural concepts. First published in 1990, the AAT covers art, architecture, decorative arts, material culture, and archival materials. Its coverage ranges from earliest times to the present day, and its scope is reported to be global. Do we, as authors of this book on image collection structures, have a problem with the AAT for use in structuring image collections? No. Do people who look at images, describe them, and attempt to find or retrieve them have problems with using only the terms included in the AAT? Yes.

The AAT, using our terminology, is simply a list of seven topics, indexed with thirty-three subtopics, which, in simplest terms, represents 231 (seven times thirty-three) categories that can be used to describe an image. Those 231 categories are further expanded to include approximately 125,000 terms that have been offered as sufficient to describe an image in a collection. Using our previously chosen image along with the AAT, we could include this O'Connor family image in an AAT-structured collection using either of the following approaches:

People   People
  People by family relationship   Groups of people
    Offspring   Social groups
      Sons   Kinship groups
                                   Families

With either of the above choices, the image could find an adequate place in a collection of family photos. However, any expression of detail one might seek for describing the action taking place would, for purposes of collection structure, be missing with the use of the AAT.

In trying to effectively and efficiently structure image collections, researchers have taken a variety of approaches recently that have directed attention to the image seeker and image viewer. Those approaches have led to additional theoretical frameworks that extend beyond the use of traditional subject headings, indexes, and thesauri for developing structure around image collections. Approaches to mapping user concepts to image document descriptions include taxonomies of various attributes, ontologies, and several sorts of metadata.

Taxonomies

Another type of list that can be used to structure an image collection is a taxonomy. In earlier times, the word *taxonomy* was used to describe the science of classifying living things, but it has since been expanded to include any system of classification that partitions a body of knowledge by creating a hierarchy of relationships among the parts. The key to constructing an effective taxonomy includes a relational hierarchy among all the terms used, with each term defining or describing one specific attribute or characteristic of the terms that precede it. The following list, using our O'Connor family photo, includes characteristics of the image, but it is not a taxonomy.

Size
Color
Location
Time

By contrast, the following, expressed as a hierarchical relationship among terms, could be considered an *image taxonomy* for photos in this collection:

Location
    Home
        Living room
        Bedroom
    College
        Dormitory room
        Cafeteria

One of the more prominent examples of an image taxonomy is the Iconclass subject-specific classification system developed in the Netherlands by H. van de Waal. It first appeared in print form in 1985 and has since become available on CD-ROM and as a Web-based service. The Iconclass is a hierarchically ordered collection of 28,000 definitions of objects, persons, events, and abstract ideas that can be the subject of an image included in works of art, reproductions, manuscript illuminations, photographs, posters, and the like.

Once again, using our O'Connor family photo and the Iconclass taxonomy, we can create yet another way to structure our photo collection, as follows:

3 Human being, man in general
    33 Relations between individual persons
        33A Nonaggressive relationships
        33B Aggressive relationships, enmity, animosity
        33C Relations between sexes

As the reader can imagine, this type of terminology, while appearing utilitarian for structuring a collection of art-related images, may not effectively portray the contents of our family collection. The other issue that arises while trying to implement a taxonomy (hierarchy of related items) to structure a collection, and similar to the issues associated with a list, index, thesaurus, or the like, is that an image may correspond (fit into) to more than one category in the structured list. Looking at the O'Connor photo and the Iconclass hierarchy, which designation would you consider to be the proper allocation of the photo in the O'Connor collection of photos? 3-33-33A, 3-33-33B, or 3-33-33C? Taxonomies may be useful, but they do not necessarily solve the problems associated with structuring an image collection.

Ontologies

Quite similar to the taxonomy is the ontology, which is another form of list from which an image collection can be structured. An *ontology* is a controlled vocabulary (similar to a thesaurus) that describes objects and the relations between them in a formal way and has a grammar for using the vocabulary terms to express something meaningful within a specified domain of interest. Ontologies can be said to resemble taxonomies, but they tend to use richer semantic relationships among the terms and attributes, and they usually use strict rules about how to specify terms and relationships. In contrast to a taxonomy, an ontology is not necessarily hierarchical but acts as a network of relationships that are used to track how items or words relate to one another. To date, most of the research work focused on image ontologies has been in specific knowledge domains, such as the biological and medical sciences, space exploration, and the expanding body of work associated with CBIR (content-based image retrieval) in relation to the colors, shapes, and textures that reside within digital images.

An example of an image ontology for the O'Connor family photos could include terms such as the following.

Image:	Name/Title/ID#
Image type:	Photos
Image class:	Immediate family
Consists of:	Images with Brian, Mary, Andrew, and/or Ethan
Stored in:	1. Albums
	2. Storage Boxes
	3. Computer Files
	4. Hanging on walls
Taken when:	January 2000 to December 2005
Used for:	1. Viewing by other family members
	2. Viewing by friends
	3. Remembering past family events
	4. Writing a book

Metadata

Metadata, in general terms, are data about data. Metadata, in the context of this discussion, can be construed as information, not *about* the contents of the image, but about how the image came to be, that is, how it was produced, size, weight (if applicable), and a host of other image attributes that have nothing to do with what is depicted in the image. For example, in referring to a painting, metadata could include information about the substrate upon which the work was painted (canvas, wood panel, etc.), the type of paint (oil, watercolor, acrylic, etc.), and who created the work and/or may have commissioned the work. If the image is a photograph, the associated metadata could include the type of camera used (including the settings), the development techniques and chemicals used, and the type of paper used to print the image. Often issues of provenance (history of ownership) are important and can also be considered metadata associated with a particular image.

The following is a list of the automatically generated metadata associated with a later image of Andrew and Mary. Images now captured in JPG format routinely include camera data as EXIF (Exchangeable Image File) that can be displayed.

Taken on
July 16, 2006 at 3.32pm CDT

Posted to Flickr
March 26, 2007 at 1.11am CDT

Edit the photo dates

Camera:	Nikon D50
Exposure:	**0.017 sec (1/60)**
Aperture:	**f/3.5**
Focal Length:	**18 mm**
Exposure Bias:	0/6 EV
Flash:	Flash fired, auto mode
ISO Speed:	400
Orientation:	Horizontal (normal)
X-Resolution:	300 dpi
Y-Resolution:	300 dpi
Software:	Ver.1.00
Date and Time:	2006:07:16 15:32:53

It is worth making the point that there is a large amount of other EXIF data contained in this image file:

- YCbCr Positioning: Co-Sited
- Date and Time (Original): 2006:07:16 15:32:53

- Date and Time (Digitized):   2006:07:16 15:32:53
- Compressed Bits per Pixel: 4 bits
- Maximum Lens Aperture: 36/10
- Metering Mode: Pattern
- Sub-Second Time: 60
- Sub-Second Time (Original):   60
- Sub-Second Time (Digitized):   60
- Color Space: sRGB
- Sensing Method: One-chip colour area sensor
- CFA Pattern: BLUE GREEN GREEN RED
- Digital Zoom Ration: 1/1
- Focal Length (35 mm equivalent):   27
- Contrast: Soft
- Compression: JPEG
- Quality: Fine
- White Balance: Auto
- Sharpening: Auto
- Focus Mode: AF-A
- Flash Setting: Normal
- Auto Flash Mode: Built-in, TTL
- Thumbnail IFD Offset: 1662
- ISO Speed Requested: 400
- Photo Corner Coordinates: 0,0,3008,2000
- AE Bracket Compensation: 0/1
- Tag::Nikon Type 3::0x001D: D50
- Tone Compensation (Contrast):   Auto
- Lens Type: 6
- Lens Focal Length, Aperture: 180/10, 550/10, 35/10, 56/10
- Flash Used: 9
- Shooting Mode: Continuous AE/Flash Bracketing Off
- White Balance: Bracketing Off
- Colour Mode: Mode 3a
- Lighting Type: SPEEDLIGHT
- Noise Reduction: OFF
- Tag::Nikon Type 3::0x009A: 78/10, 78/10
- Tag::Nikon Type 3::0x00A2:   2853664
- Total Number of Shutter Releases: 3489
- Saturation: Normal
- Digital Vari-Program: AUTO
- Image Width: 3,008 pixels
- Image Height: 2,000 pixels

Those in control or in authority over an image collection usually determine the metadata required for the collection. Often, however, those requirements are selected without regard for the needs of the viewing audience and function merely as extraneous bits of information that clutter the information landscape surrounding the image. Most professionals who are tasked with metadata development and implementation for image collections take extreme care in relation to what the general public has rights to access. Many times, controlling interests in a valuable collection of images will be reluctant to divulge any metadata that provide information about the cost of the item, where it came from, and in some cases where it is kept.

With the advent of digital imagery and the proliferation of online image databases, the metadata attached to an image can be quite extensive. In some cases, we would argue, the metadata system has outweighed the importance of more critical access points to the collection that would give image seekers more flexibility for finding the images they might need.

Templates

A template is another form of list that establishes or serves as a pattern. In that sense, an image collection can be structured along the lines of a template in order to facilitate access to collection viewers. The literature on this subject is sparse, which points again to one of our main issues: words can act to both segregate as well as integrate concepts. The word *template* could initially be assumed to be one more way to structure an image collection; yet templates (as posed initially by information studies professor Corrine Jorgensen in the 1990s) are intended to act as search *patterns* for finding images in a collection more efficiently.

Regardless of collection structure, Jorgensen points out that image retrieval is mostly a function of identifying the object(s) depicted. However, image seekers may want to search for photos using other attributes, some that are specific physical attributes and some that are conceptual. For example, some may seek images that tell a story, depict relationships among people, include specific colors, match a particular theme, or generate a specific personal reaction. All in all, Jorgensen identified forty-eight such image attributes. She has since concluded that no single attribute outweighs another as a pattern for image retrieval. Although Jorgensen justly calls for professionals to consider these attributes when creating structure around an image collection, a missing element is that viewers do not use the same words to describe the same images and thus will not necessarily be well served, even with more categories for image-retrieval purposes.

Typologies

A *typology* is the result of the classification of things according to a shared characteristic or characteristics. Any image collection can be structured around a set of typologies, which is similar to creating a list of the topics that are in the collection. Typologies are a very common approach for collection hobbyists. For example, a collection of baseball card images is most likely separated into topics by team name and location, that is, Chicago Cubs, New York Yankees, etc. No image can appear in more than one typology. Stamp collectors, coin collectors, postcard collectors, and others each tend to establish typologies by which the image items in the collections can be easily identified and accessed. A typical typology, albeit incomplete, for a set of family photos might be as follows:

> When We Were Young
> College Years
> Our Wedding
> The Kids
> Special Events
> Vacations

Of course, typologies are not without their problems as well. Would the birth of a new family member go with The Kids or with Special Events? Should Vacations be subdivided into photos by location (Boston, London, etc.) or by type of vacation (city, seashore, mountains, cruises)?

Typologies are fairly easy to create but may tend to play havoc with collection structure as more and more additions are made and as ready access to specific images becomes a blurred vision across overlapping topics. In a recent discussion with a professional graphic designer of Web sites and collateral print materials, the question was asked: "How do you structure the collection of images that you use?" The immediate response was: "I keep them in computer folders by name of the client." The question was then put forward: "As your client list grows, how will you remember which folder contains a particular image." The response was: "Most of the photos are rights managed, so, in most cases, I only use particular images for the same client." Being persistent, the following question was posed: "But if you wanted to find a specific image that you used for a specific client that you worked for several years ago, would you be able to access it?" Her answer was: "I think so, I have a good memory."

The success of a typology for structuring an image collection lies in its ability to expand the memory of its users, not to rely on it. If the tags used are too general, the ultimate lament becomes, "I know I have that picture here somewhere, I just can't seem to locate it."

Topic Maps

A more recent approach to using topics for descriptive purposes and as an aid for representing information and its retrieval is the topic map. Topic maps use concepts, associations (which represent the relationships between them), and occurrences (which represent relationships between topics and information resources relevant to them). They are similar to semantic networks, which were first invented for computers in the 1950s. Topic maps can be constructed from linguistic components, which again points to another method of using words to describe and access images in a collection.

Meronymy (A is part of B; steering wheel is part of automobile)

Holonymy (B has A as a part of itself; automobiles have wheels, brakes, etc)

Hyponymy (A is subordinate of B; automobile is subordinate to transportation)

Hypernymy (A is superordinate of B; automobile is superordinate to sedan)

Synonymy (A denotes the same as B; automobile is the same as car)

Returning to our O'Connor photo, we could construct a topic map that could be used to structure an image collection and facilitate access to similar concepts, associations, and occurrences, as follows.

Topics	Associations	Occurrences
Brian	Took photographs	Web site
Andrew	Visited at college	Picture frame
Mary	Involved in dorm room antics	Photo album

By using a topic map structure, several relationships can be identified for use in both accessing and retrieving this image:

1. Brian "took photograph" of Andrew and Mary
2. Mary and Brian "visited (Andrew) at college"
3. Andrew was "involved in dorm room antics" in view of Brian and Mary

From such a topic map, we could structure the collection of which this photo is a part as follows:

1. Photographs taken by Brian
2. Photographs taken while visiting Andrew at college
3. Photographs of dorm room antics
4. Photographs of Andrew and Mary

The creation of topic maps is much more tedious that creating a typology, yet both have their advantages and disadvantages. A topic map structure assumes that underlying associations exist among the images in the collection, whereas a typology normally is created to encompass as many topics as possible to give structure to the collection whether associations exist among those topics or not.

We hope that by discussing these various approaches for structuring image collections, we have enabled the reader to grasp the arduous nature of supplying just the right words for adequately describing, explaining, and accessing an image in a collection of images. If indeed, an image can be worth a thousand words, which words will best serve the intent of your collection and ensure access to it? The preceding chapters illustrate that the elements of an image, along with the elements of language, can combine to undermine simple, unified accounts of image content, particularly from the point of view of image collection structure. We do not mean to end on a negative note; however, the complexities of applying descriptors to photographs and queries for photographs are numerous and vexing. Sensitivity to such complexities is necessary for image retrieval system designers and users.

CHAPTER NINE

"TAG, YOU'RE IT!"

Kilroy was here. after James J. Kilroy, a shipyard inspector from Massachusetts, who, after completing his inspection of a ship or plane, would mark his work.

I N THIS ONGOING discussion surrounding structures of image collections, the recurring thread has been a focus on ways that images can be classified (using words) so that their location in a collection can be accessed and a particular image viewed. Up to this point, each of the approaches to classification that have been mentioned involved some form of faceted classification. A facet, in its simplest sense, is a category. But, more importantly, facets are the various categories into which a given class of items or objects can be divided. For example, the class "photographs" can be divided into facets (categories) that have characteristics that make them part of the photograph class, such as the following:

Daguerreotype	Ambrotype	Calotype
Carte-de-visite	Gum bichromate	Heliograph
Salted paper print	Stereograph	Tintype
Albumen print	Gelatin print	Instant color print
Digital photo		

While each of these facets can be placed in a class called photographs, each facet itself can be a class that maintains its own facets, such as

Digital photos
   JPEG images
   GIF images
   TIF images
   PNG images

Whether list, index, directory, catalogue, thesaurus, taxonomy, ontology, template, or topic map, some form of faceted classification is involved that uses words to describe images in order to organize them and create structure around the collection. Recent developments resulting in the enhanced storage capacity of computer files, the increased speed of access to images in large databases, and the transparency associated with Internet access to a multitude of image-related materials have spawned additional approaches for accessing and retrieving items from an image collection that tend to ignore the facets normally associated with a class of images.

Two of the most used approaches (outside of automated, content-based retrieval methods) at the time of this publishing are browsing and tagging. Neither of these frameworks for accessing images in a collection can be considered a collection structure, but each can be considered when a collection is being built in order to make that collection more versatile in terms of image access to collection viewers.

BROWSING

Browsing, by definition, is glancing in a casual way. Browsing, in the context of image retrieval, can be defined as glancing in a focused way. The issue at hand is whether the eye can glance and focus at the same time. The authors believe that it happens every time someone says: "I'm not quite sure what I want, but I'll know it when I see it."

Browsing, as a theoretical framework for enhanced image retrieval, has been described and cited since the 1980s in a variety of professional venues involved with the development of better methods for querying database systems that house collections of images. Most professional photographers and photojournalists will recall browsing an image collection using a light box, an enclosure containing white light behind a flat translucent glass or plastic surface on which transparencies or negatives are laid in order to examine them. In essence, the light box is a tool for selecting the best, least-flawed, most meaningful images for an assignment. That concept has since been transposed to the Internet in the form of "thumbnails" on a Web page. Anyone who has used an image search engine on the Web has experienced the thumbnail light box. Those pages, with anywhere from ten to one hundred thumbnails per page, are placed there for your browsing pleasure, to select the best, least-flawed, most meaningful image for your current need (copyright issues aside).

Why do we say "browsing" and not "viewing and selecting"? To date, most image search engines are word-matching tools that can only retrieve images that match the words in a keyword query of the image database. If an image seeker is looking for a specific image or type of image, he or she must enter words that will allow access to the images that are being sought. If the image seeker knows exactly what is needed, the unresolved issue is whether the exact words are entered to ensure that the need will be fulfilled. Often the exact need is returned by the query, but it is not available immediately and is sequestered four, ten, fifty, or one hundred Web pages of images later. To discover the exact need becomes a process of browsing. And this is often an arduous task involving extreme patience.

Efficient browsing depends on some plan of action for conducting the search. That plan can be algorithmic or heuristic, depending on the mindset of the individual image seeker. The plan of action is quite important in terms of collection structure. Most approaches to technology-based image retrieval systems impose a set of algorithms that an image seeker must abide by because that is the way the system has been programmed.

An algorithm sets specific boundaries around the search parameters, which in and of themselves set an algorithmic threshold for the search. In other words, keywords based on a controlled vocabulary impose algorithmic constraints that an image seeker's browsing heuristics attempt to overcome. A *heuristic* is an unstructured plan in which each step taken acts as a new beginning for the next step and, if successful, may or may not work the next time. For example, driving the quickest, shortest route to work is an algorithmic process; finding that route is a heuristic process.

Browsing heuristics are somewhat unique to every information seeker, whether the search involves textual material or image-related material. We each have a tendency to browse through materials using different patterns of browsing behavior depending on the task at hand, the time available, and the effort we are willing to expend.

Current research being conducted on methods to improve the nature of *browsing sets* of images has provided some interesting avenues for enhancing the image-retrieval process, but so far, the methods still rely on underlying frameworks based on word searching for terms attached to an image in a database. If the image seeker does not use the exact words, proper language, and plausible concepts, the same issues and problems arise in the image-retrieval process to which we have become accustomed and to which we have referred in our prior chapters.

Researchers also are investigating approaches to browsing sets that involve images only (no words); however, as already mentioned, most if not all of these methods focus on the colors, shapes, and textures in the image, not the concepts with which the image can be associated. This major difference has created a bifurcated research arena composed of content-based researchers and concept-based researchers. To date, there have been few attempts and even fewer successes in merging these two approaches to enhance image collection structure and retrieval, especially for large image databases with diverse sets of images.

From comments about images in memory made by Miller and Johnson-Laird in *Language and Perception*, we further posit as a synthesis of their assertions that image searching is a complex skill under the influence of higher-order cognitive processing in which some words evoke images more readily than others, and considering that humans have some level of voluntary control over the features of an image they attend to, searching is almost purely a matter of controlling attention to particular features. We assume, therefore, that some part of the mental encoding of a specific feature in memory is a "tag" that helps people distinguish that feature from other features in the same image and helps them distinguish one image from others that resemble it.

Browsing, in that context, is a search tied to a specific or unspecified need that links mentally aroused tags with the search items under investigation. In the case of image search and retrieval, that investigation can be just a glance at a thumbnail image that is appended to the matching tags that link the searcher's need to his or her cognitive forethought to an image at hand.

TAGGING

The concept of tagging as it relates to collection structure is not new. Its roots extend back to classical Greece and the Roman Empire, when individuals would make "their mark" or scratch their inscriptions on walls, which we have come to know today as graffiti. The word *tag* and the act of tagging came into prominence after World War II when urban gangs would use a unique sign, symbol, or signature to mark what they considered to be their exclusive territory. In the 1960s the idea of tagging made its debut in the news media in New York City when a street messenger, spray can in hand, tagged his "TAKI 183" signature on streets, subway stations, and subway cars throughout the city. Today, graffiti tags are still prominent in almost every major city around the world, and we are now starting to see tags on the Internet associated with Web pages and image collections.

One of the more popular and predominant sites that uses the tagging concept is the Flickr Web site. Flickr was originally developed by a Canada-based company and launched in 2004 as a multi-user chat room with real-time photo exchange capabilities. As the Web site continued to evolve, it focused more on uploading and storing user images, and as of this writing, Flickr allows photo submitters to categorize their images by using keyword tags for easy access to images on certain topics or subject matter. In addition, the site allows users to categorize their photos into sets (groups of photos) that are more flexible than the traditional folder concept that most of us have become accustomed to for storing our photos in a computer-based environment. The more unique aspect of the tag that has found favor on the Flickr site is the use of *tag clouds*. The tag cloud is simply an assembly of verbal descriptors that define the more popularly used tags that make up the entire Flickr database of user photos. The larger the font in the tag cloud, the more popular is the use of that tag among current users. A tag cloud looks like this:

> animal, **art**, beach, black, bird, canada, **family**, flowers, **friends**, honeymoon, . . .

One of the major values of tagging is its nonhierarchical nature. Key-word categorization can be applied freely based on the cognitive connection between viewer and viewing object. This concept has been further advanced by another popular Web site, at http://del.icio.us. The del.icio.us site describes itself as a social bookmarking Web site designed to allow users to store and share their favorite bookmarks on the Web instead of in their individual browsers. For example, if the keyword "da Vinci" was entered into the del.icio.us search dialogue box, the results would supply access to some of the following sites that other del.icio.us users have found useful or intriguing:

> The Drawings of Leonardo da Vinci (saved by 548 people using the following keywords: art, drawing, history, davinci, science)
>
> Leonardo da Vinci's 10 Best Ideas (saved by 89 people using the following keywords: science, history, davinci, technology, inventions)
>
> Leonardo da Vinci: Qualities of a Genius and How to Think Productively (saved by 365 people using the following keywords: creativity, productivity, thinking, life hacks, genius)

The designers of this site infer that tagging can be a lot easier and more flexible than fitting information into preconceived categories or folders, which raises the question: Should major institutions allow visitors to their Web site to tag their important and valued holdings that are available for Web viewing? Would such tagging provide a greater number of access points to those holdings and thus increase the visibility of the institution and its holdings? We do not propose such an idea, but merely suggest that tools currently exist, such as tagging and tag clouds, that can enhance the quality of an online collection of images based on the public's being given access to those collections.

CLADISTICS

In the biological sciences, *cladistics* is a method of hypothesizing relationships among organisms. Like other methods, it has its own terminology, sets of assumptions, procedures, and limitations. As we continue our discussion on the structures of image collections, it is interesting to note how cladistic analysis parallels similar concepts for uncovering and identifying relationships among images. If we take the basic idea from cladistics that members of a group are closely related more so to some members of the group than others, we can synthesize a similar methodology in association with the organization of image collections by restating the three basic assumptions of cladistic analysis:

1. Any group of images can be related by a characteristic, feature, or attribute in common.

2. The application of language can be used to introduce bifurcating patterns among those images for use in structuring the collection.
3. When the choice of language applications is changed, the characteristics, features, and/or attributes in common, when applied to the same set of images, can change, altering the relationships within that set of images and thus changing the structure of the collection.

The first assumption can apply to any collection of images regardless of size and contents. This assumption states that, with all the diversity that exists among the features, characteristics, and attributes of an image collection, there is always some overarching relationship that ties all of the images together into one collection. For example: The John J. Audubon Collection.

The second assumption says that from one (set of images), there is always a way to linguistically bifurcate into two (or more sets of images) based on the language, grammar, and syntax being used. Language can always be used to turn a homogeneous collection into a heterogeneous collection. For example: Audubon Birds and Audubon Quadrupeds.

The third assumption is the most important in using a cladistic approach to establishing relationships among images. In traditional cladistic analysis, the convention is to call the original state of the characteristic *pleisiomorphic* (a primitive characteristic of the group under consideration) and the derived state the *apomorphic* (derived from the original state). For example, the above collections of birds and quadrupeds (the primitive states of the collection) could just as easily be reassembled into apomorphic or derived states that could include Audubon Carnivores and Audubon Herbivores, with each subcollection containing both birds and quadrupeds.

It should be noted that in the examples listed above, a structured collection may emerge from a linguistic bifurcation of the collection items using a cladistic style of approach. Our intent with this discourse is not to promote this type of approach for the organization of all image collections; however, we are endeavoring to show that image collection structure not only is based on the organizing authority residing with the collector, but also is a function of the cognitive authority inherent in the viewer. In the examples above, each structure offers different points of access to the collection that extends beyond traditional subject-heading approaches through broad term (BT), near term (NT), and related term (RT) terminology.

Even more important to this discussion is to remember that this type of cladistic approach allows the collection to be approached entirely as a "derived from" hypothesis in lieu of the traditional approach of structuring from the primitive elements of the collected images. We offer the following collection of images for the reader to ponder in the context of primitive relationships versus relationships derived from the viewing experience.

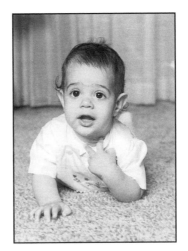

How many collections? Using what primitive elements? Derived from what?

CHAPTER TEN

MOVING ON

Machines were mice and men were lions once upon a time, but now that it's the opposite, it's twice upon a time.

Moondog

TWO COLLECTIONS THAT AREN'T THAT ARE

We open this chapter with an odd title and lovely quote from musician Moondog, to set the stage for a consideration of two nearly opposite examples of *collection* and *structure* in hopes of stretching our notions of the two concepts. First, we will consider the movies; then we will consider individual ultra-high-resolution still images.

Movies arose from a history of entertainment, engineering, and science. They also arose from still pictures. In fact, a movie is nothing more (or less) than a sequence of still images with one primary structuring attribute—presentation of a set of still images to the viewer at a fixed rate. For the video media available these days, that rate is 30 frames per second. Actually, the presentation rate is 29.97 frames per second, to allow for certain housekeeping necessities in maintaining the constant frame rate. This means that every one minute of viewing time is made up of 1,800 still images.

There is no constraint on what those frames should be for any given video, only that they should be presented at 30 frames per second if the illusion of life-like motion is to be maintained. Giving a

Photo by Mary K. O'Connor.

viewer 1,800 still images, even if they were printed from the frames of the film, would not result in an illusion of motion. In order to be a movie, the bunch of images must be structured in such a way as to be presentable at 30 frames per second. The illustration here is a small portion of the frames

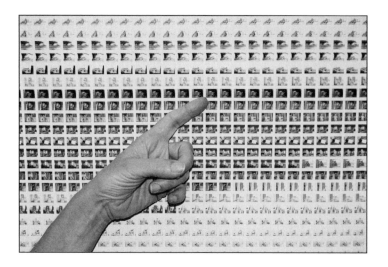

from a motion picture. All of the 12,803 frames from a 7.1-minute section of the movie are printed on a large sheet of paper. They make for a nice poster and they are not without use, but they are not a movie.

Whether the recording device is a film camera, an analog video camera, or a digital video camera, it is a device that records many still images rapidly. It is not a device that records motion. It is a device that records fragments of motion. In fact, there is a significant amount of time in which it is not recording anything, even when running.

That is to say, this sort of collection of images functions as a movie if and only if playback occurs at the prescribed frame rate. The structural element is temporal. This is not to say that the collection cannot be used in other ways. Football coaches have made a significantly different use of movies for decades by violating the temporal element—stopping the film at the moment a particularly good or bad move was recorded, reversing the film and playing a short

sequence over again and again, or moving fast-forward through portions that are not relevant for the particular segment of the team watching the film. Police, athletic coaches, and film theorists all routinely look at some portions of film or video footage in slow motion or even frame-by-frame, looking for a particular momentary piece of data or a particular discontinuity in the data. High-speed recording of numerous frames (perhaps hundreds or even

thousands of frames per second) enables playback at very slow motion and, thus, analysis of a large number of data points per second. On the whole, the filmic collection of frames is structured such that it only functions when played back at a standard rate.

Let us now think about the production and viewing processes to see if we can tease out other structures. Let us look briefly at the film construction process, then at the film viewing process. Here we will use the example of a documentary film on a rodeo. There is no particular reason for this choice, except that documentaries generally fall between the individually produced home movie or artistic piece and the large production-team construction of a Hollywood feature.

The filmmaker engages in one or more photocutionary acts. Either by preplanning or by making decisions at the moment of recording, the filmmaker gathers together a collection of images at the rodeo. The content of those images—both topic and production values—will have been guided by the filmmaker's plan for the collection, as well as by the filmmaker's understanding of the intended audience. That is, if the filmmaker wants to present the human

athletic ability of rodeo riders, then the majority of images in the collection will be constructed to give more frame space to the riders than to the horses, clowns, or audience. If, on the other hand, the filmmaker intends an ethnographic study of the rituals surrounding rodeo, then there will likely be many images showing, behind-the-scenes preparations, audience members reacting to events, announcers, clowns, and all the other participants.

After all the images have been made, they will be arranged. Some of the original images will likely be discarded for poor technical quality, duplication, inappropriateness for the revised plan for the film, length considerations, or any of myriad other artistic and logistical reasons. The filmmaker may choose to leave the images in more or less chronological order or to rearrange the images to suit the plan of the film. There is no "grammar" of film in the sense of a verbal grammar. There is no analog to the noun or verb. This does not mean that there are no structures to movies; far from it. However, the structures are built on the filmmaker's understanding of viewer perception. Filmmakers learned long ago that structure is a powerful component; they also learned that there is no one-to-one correspondence of filmic structural practices to verbal structural practices. There are some tried-and-true structural practices, such as using "fast" editing to increase excitement. However, there are other methods of achieving excitement, and the rapid intercutting of dull or inappropriate images will not achieve excitement.

So the filmmaker carries out photocutionary acts at the image gathering and image ordering stages. In a general sense, the filmmaker also conducts photocutionary acts at the showing stage by determining the type of recording and distribution mechanisms (for example, wide release in theaters, showings for a few friends, direct release to DVD). Likewise, the viewer carries out several photocutionary acts. The most evident is the choice to view a particular work. Once upon a time, the collection of movies was limited to whatever came to the local theater. Film viewing was passive at many levels, not the least of which was that the collection came in bits and pieces and did not accumulate (the reels for last week's film were on their way to another town). In some communities, public libraries had small collections of films, generally of the sort used in schools. Now, of course, it is quite the opposite. Between multiplex theaters in most municipalities, multiple video rental outlets, cable television, video-on-demand, video on the Web, and video on numerous personal portable devices, the collection of videos is enormous and is no longer ephemeral. So simply choosing a movie document is now an active photocutionary act.

In the past, watching a movie in a theater or a television show at home was a passive experience in which the images went by in their prescribed order and at the prescribed rate. When the movie ended, that was the end of the viewing act unless one paid for another viewing or waited for reruns. Now reruns are easier to find and there is a large array of time-shifting devices and practices. Viewers also have the ability to directly and actively engage in the viewing process. The ability to rewind, speed ahead, or play one segment over and over is now no longer available only to producers and a few privileged users (athletic coaches, law enforcement officers, scientists)

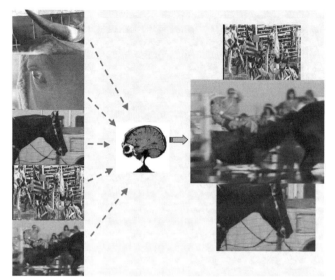

whose work enabled them to purchase expensive playback machinery. Videotape, then various digital media, have made it possible for virtually any user to view the collection of still images making up the movie in almost any manner they like. For the majority of situations, the standard playback rate is still the default mode, but examination and reexamination of individual frames and sets of frames is not only possible but also essentially trivial to achieve.

In either case, whether simple passive viewing or highly interactive viewing, photocutionary acts are taking place. In the passive single viewing, it is unlikely that most viewers of a half-hour documentary or a two-hour feature film will recall every image in its prescribed order. Some images will be more striking and more memorable; some will be remembered out of context or out of order; some will likely be misremembered. After the viewing, there will be, in effect, another collection of images. This one will be the viewer's collection, constructed and arranged by the viewer's individual criteria.

So we might say of a movie that it is, in the most general model, a collection of still images structured first and foremost by the mechanical necessities of reproduction. The actual number of still images is large—1,800 frames per minute of viewing time. Ordinarily, a viewer comes to such a collection to see the whole collection, not simply a few particular images. We might say that a moving image document is a collection of images that is intended to be viewed as a single document, so it pushes the boundaries of the definition of a collection—a collection of one.

Let us turn then to a companion case—the single image that contains multiple "documents" or ways of being seen. For this we turn to ultra-high-resolution digital photography and the sensibilities of the surrealists. Of necessity, we will discuss the work of a particular photographer whose images embody this combination of high-resolution and surrealist vision. Artist Benjamin Blackwell was a highly regarded surrealist painter who shifted into the photographic medium. Much of his personal work has the overt look of snapshots, but upon deeper inspection, we see that his work demonstrates how a single image may present a collection of images. Using high resolution means that portions of an image can be snatched from a larger whole and still be of sufficient resolution to fulfill typical uses of photographs. However, grabbing several discrete portions of a large photo-graph is only a superficial sense of several images in one.

Let us refresh our memories with a few quotes on surrealism.

> For Surrealists, photographs were full of meanings that resulted from the intersection of unexpected happenings, and the artist's objective was to stimulate the emotions with the element of surprise. (p. 188)

> Kertesz called himself a "naturalist Surrealist" because of his skill at recording a scene as he found it. (p. 173)

> The removal of an everyday object from its expected context was a favorite strategy of the Surrealist art practiced by René Magritte. (p. 153)
>
> W. Naef. *The J. Paul Getty Museum Handbook of the Photographs Collections*

Andre Breton, in his 1934 lecture "What Is Surrealism?" described surrealism, in part, as "Transmutation of those two seemingly contradictory states, dream and reality, into a sort of absolute reality, of surreality, so to speak."

Surrealism as a movement sought to break down the distinction between the rational and trained engagements with ideas and the world and other modes of engagement; it sought integration of more ways of modeling human relationships with the environment in its largest sense. Efforts to achieve a surrealistic state often involved surprise or unexpected combina-tions of elements.

We might look to Naef's comment on Magritte and suggest that almost any photograph "remove[s] an everyday object from its expected context." Digital photos go in both directions—making the photo itself an everyday object and an expected context on the one hand (cell phone) and, on the other hand, images made with ultra-high resolution cameras that yield more data than we ordinarily see.

If I pick up a photograph of my son while I am sitting at my keyboard, I have in my hand a representation ripped from its temporal and spatial con-text. My son is more than one foot tall; he operates within at least three dimensions; he has a scent about him; he ages. In the photograph in my hand, he never ages; the stimuli striking my eyes reengage the same neural pathways that his body did several years ago. This photograph is not a win-dow on the world, so much as it is a two-dimensional projection of a three-dimensional moment in time. At the moment of my seeing the photograph, my son is not on the cross-country race course, he does not have blonde hair, his smile is no longer so youthful.

Perhaps the snapshot is for us so ordinary, so abundant, that it no longer seems to embody an unexpected event. In the case of the photograph of my son, it is one of hundreds or even thousands of photographs made of him in his twenty-three years. Yet, upon reflection, it is surely unexpected, in at least some senses, that my seventeen-year-old son is now in my office beaming a radiant smile; at the same time, my rational self "knows" that he is twenty-three years old and is two thousand miles away living a life often quite separate from me.

This ripping out of context, the surprise, the naturalist surrealism arising from the skill of recording a scene as found reaches some form of zenith in the ultra-high-resolution photographs made possible by Ben Blackwell's Better Light. Better Light manufactures hardware and software that enable some of the highest-resolution imaging available. Blackwell has mastered techniques of presenting stimulus sets to the eyes of viewers that closely resemble what the original objects would present to eyes. Yet they also present qualities surprisingly at odds with visual expectations.

Blackwell's photographs of buildings are, at first, striking because they look so like snapshots; indeed, they often appear to be snapshots of rather prosaic buildings or odd little buildings that serve prosaic functions. In the ice cream shop photo, a building crafted to resemble an ice cream cone is presented dead center, in violation of ordinary rules of composition. There are no people, no intriguing event takes place, no dramatic clouds draw the eye upward. Just an odd little building set right in the middle with a vertical utility pole and a horizontal red curbing adding to the rectilinear snapshot character of the image.

However, the three elements of centrality, rectilinear framing, and lack of drama begin to take this image beyond even the posited surreality of the snapshot. The horizontal curb line is consciously placed just above the bottom frame line, not simply an unnoticed element in front of the lens of someone recording just the cute building. While many snapshots have a centrality—perhaps because of autofocusing mechanisms normally operating in the center of the frame; perhaps because snapshot shooters simply care to make sure their primary object is shown in full—Blackwell's image is so perfectly centered that it gives the impression of being perfectly balanced, solid.

Blackwell thus combines the seeming ordinary nature of the snapshot with careful craft and, ultimately, a surrealist artistry. The application of years of technical training and many thousands of dollars worth of equipment are at odds with the ordinary experience of snapping a picture as one walks or drives by an ordinary scene. The very precision of the composition and technique behind the making of the image bespeaks a lack of the spontaneity of a snapshot—often indicated by tilted framing, not-quite-centered subject, family or friends standing in front.

It might be suggested that another element is causing an unexpected reaction. The centrality and the secondary framing of the utility pole and curbing invite or compel repeated viewing both in and of themselves and in the "not-quite-rightness" of a snapshot that does not stimulate in the manner of a snapshot. In addition, the exposure is "perfect"—it has more dynamic range than the typical snapshot. There is detail in shadows at the same time that highlights are not "blown out." Human eyes can span a large dynamic range, but not in a single view without adjustment over time. In that sense, the viewer is presented with a representation of a single slice of time that could not be seen by a human eye in that same small slice of time. This would be more "obvious" in a time exposure of automobile headlights at night, or in an Ansel Adams image of mountains and clouds—an image in a place out of the ordinary with a good deal of technical manipulation.

The uncommon subject and lighting signal themselves and so do not present themselves as the "intersection of unexpected happenings" (surrealism). The highly crafted snapshot, precisely by not announcing its specialness, presents us with a discord that bespeaks an intersection—subtle, yet still an intersection.

Surreality could be argued on the basis of composition and craft alone, but another characteristic of the ultra-high-resolution recording medium brings about a different, heightened form of "removal of an everyday object from its expected context." In the process of making unmediated views of the world, we are quite capable of and accustomed to seeing the large "picture" and the details; however, this ordinarily requires some change of perspective, such as walking closer. That is, the picture viewing experience has a conscious engagement and temporal component. The ultra-high-resolution image presents the big picture and the details all at once. This is not to say that the image as a whole and all the details can be attended to without some form of engagement or a change of engagement; however, the amount of distance and the length of the time component are (potentially) significantly reduced. Instead of having to stand across the street to see the large image of the ice cream shop and then having to walk across the street to read the prices, the viewer of the photograph need only turn his or her eyes or head, or perhaps walk one or two steps to one side or the other. Again, this is a subtle intersection of the unexpected.

We must remember that it is not at all unusual to see prints of photographs that are measured in feet rather than inches. What we are talking

about in the work of Ben Blackwell is the intersection of imaging technology capable of producing large prints with extraordinary detail—much more than in the typical advertising poster, for example—with an extraordinary sense for representing the extraordinary, the surreal, in the ordinary.

In one small study of viewer engagement with ultra-high-resolution photographs, we asked Blackwell to photograph one of the walls in my office—variously described as high entropy, or messy. The resulting image is shown above in three instantiations: a fragment with someone viewing; a "standard-size" print, and a longer view of the entire image in scale with the person in the image. The image required approximately two hours of setup time for composition, lighting (natural window light controlled by blinds and fluorescent tubes, all balanced by software manipulation), lens selection, and other arcana of the craft.

We conducted some formal experiments with the image to determine, first, how people would look at the images—given a choice, they would stand ten feet back, then walk up and spend a long time looking at details; second, how much they would remember—more than those who saw the standard-size print; and third, how they felt about the viewing experience—"entranced" by the detail and by having a "whole collection of images" in one print. Of course, habituation to such high-resolution images would likely reduce the sense of entrancement, but the sense of having multiple images within one print would likely remain.

More relevant to the concept of surreality was a set of observations of two dozen doctoral-level information scientists crawling around on their hands and knees to examine a set of Blackwell images of various buildings. We needed a large, impromptu venue, so we put the images on the floor outside a conference meeting room in a hotel. The anecdotal evidence was of a fascination with what looked like snapshots, or "mere records," that just "were off"—this was evidently a technical term for the intersection of unexpected happenings. A few of the images did have people or other moving elements that cause interesting effects in the images, because the digital technology requires long exposure times rather more like those of the photography of the nineteenth century. So discussion did, at times, turn to calculations of four-dimensional attributes, with time being the fourth dimension. Yet, over the course of an hour, the primary engagement by the vast majority of scientists was a fascination with the unexpected combination of the snapshot appearance with color, light, and resolution characteristics that were different from snapshots by orders of magnitude.

So we might posit that the notions of composition, dynamic range, and compression of time and distance into a high-resolution image present to the viewer an intersection, a removal from the ordinary, a recording of the scene "as found" but not merely through a window. All these notions give

Blackwell's photographs a surreal quality made all the more compelling by the surface-level lack of artifice combined with characteristics at odds with that lack of artifice. That naïve viewers and information scientists could not take their eyes off the images (as many of them said) lends credence to this thesis. Blackwell achieves the disruption, the intersection, and the removal of context (often of the viewer rather than the viewed) with a subtlety and engagement in the best (most provocative) manner of the surrealists.

So, in much the same manner that we presented the moving image document as a large number of images that acted as a single document, we suggest that single ultra-high-resolution photographs can act as collections of multiple viewing possibilities. It would not take much to argue that some of the same things could be said of any individual photograph. Merely by ripping an object out of its native time and place and presenting it as a two-dimensional object of study, even an ordinary snapshot made with a low-re-solution camera and little or no thought to production values may present us with a surrealist document—a weaving together of reality and dreaming.

PART IV

GROUPTHINK, DEINDIVIDUATION, AND DESENSITIVITY

Individuality: The total character peculiar to and distinguishing an individual from others.

Merriam-Webster's Online

The phenomenology of perception as put forth by Merleau-Ponty says that seeing an image before unseen conjures an interpretation rooted in past experience, whether the one interpreting is the image creator, collector, curator, or curious viewer. If there are characteristics in common among those various interpretations, it is often mere coincidence. As such, meaning does not reside in the image. It resides in the beholder. Hence, thresholds of meaning are approached through interpretation because the image itself makes no statements, and those statements of interpretation arise from neither knowledge nor ignorance. They arise from experience.

From this premise, we argue that current frameworks for structuring image collections tend to promote a measure of forced conformity that is not necessarily a stable characteristic of visual experience. As suggested by psychologist Irving Janis in 1972, people can be susceptible to "groupthink" when they conform their opinions to what they believe to be the consensus of the group making the decisions. Images that reside in collections that are already "labeled" with titles, descriptions, and keywords for ready accessibility enforce this type of groupthink on unsuspecting viewers. Be advised that this posture is not intended to insult the learned professionals who have spent literally hundreds of thousands of hours trying to educate the public with descriptive material of and about the images in their collections. Our lament is that most image collections, both public and private, are structured around passive viewers, whose individual reactions, interpretations, and responses are deemed ineffectual byproducts for enhancing access to and understanding of the adjunct properties and characteristics inherent in both the image and the collection. The so-called masterpieces in any collection are normalized through repetition as viewers are subjugated to norms of appearance, sometimes propagandized historical reference, and artificial values bolstered by naïve publics and competition among societal elitists. This point of view can be attested to by a trip to the Louvre and a visit with da Vinci's *Mona Lisa*. The size of the painting is not impressive, the subject matter is mundane, the style is reflective of the period, yet throngs of visitors line up to get a peek in order to say: "I saw it!"

GROUPTHINK

Groupthink is a concept that was identified by Irving Janis in his 1972 publication of *Victims of Groupthink*. The premise derives from attempts at group cohesiveness and agreement that result in faulty decision making. Groups experiencing groupthink do not consider all alternatives and seek unanimity at the expense of quality decisions. The value of groupthink concepts in the context of this discussion is that "tradition" tends to undermine creative thinking and the avoidance of alternative ideas and solutions. And by saying *tradition*, we are referring to the fact that the basis for structuring most approaches to organizing image collections is rooted in text-bound bibliographic rules, policies, and procedures. If text is removed from the image equation, the total character of an image is able to emerge unscathed, allowing it to merge or diverge from other images that may reside in a collection. For example, if we return to the images in chapter 3, we can demonstrate our viewpoint:

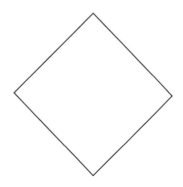

Groupthink would tell us that these images should have a specific designation and location in a collection. To accomplish such an organizing task would require that some textual concept be applied to merge these images (four-sided figures, polygons, right-angled diagrams, etc.) or separate them into divergent categories (square-shaped, diamond-shaped, grey figures, white figures, etc.). Once that textual assignment has been made for an image, we have deindividuated the image.

DEINDIVIDUATION

Deindividuation theory is rooted in the earliest works of social psychology, in particular Gustave Le Bon's (1895–1995) crowd theory. The field of social psychology revived Le Bon's ideas in the 1950s and couched them in more scientific terms as a theory of deindividuation. Initially, it was argued that deindividuation occurs when individuals in a group are not paid attention to as individuals. Thus, being unaccountable in a crowd or group has the psychological consequence of reducing inner restraints, and increasing behavior that is usually inhibited.

In relation to images in a structured collection, we would argue that deindividuation occurs at two levels: (1) the image level, and (2) the viewer level. At the image level, information surrounding an image as to its creation, background, provenance, or value removes the true character of the image resulting from a strict sense of visual engagement. As a result, the "crowd" of images is deindividuated, because each image is not paid attention to but is only considered as one of a like group that offers the same content, qualities, or characteristics. At the viewer level, deindividuation occurs when a viewer may "ooh and aah" in the crowd surrounding a famous painting but remain constrained and inhibited in front of another painting about which the viewer knows nothing, around which no crowds are in evidence, even though the viewer likes or enjoys viewing this painting even more.

DESENSITIVITY

We consider desensitivity as a third impediment to more creative approaches to image collection structure. By desensitivity we refer to the implication that language is the most appropriate avenue for creating structure around seeking, searching, retrieving, displaying, and storing image collections. Although some inroads have been made for improving image retrieval through content-based approaches (color, shape, texture), image collectors and image viewers have been *desensitized* to anything other than key descriptors and keywords to communicate their likes, dislikes, and critical opinions of visual experiences. Until the image itself is able to supply avenues of

communication, we believe that further advancements in collection struc-
ture(s) remain somewhat curtailed.

Recognizing that these arguments border on the esoteric, we conclude
this introduction to part IV by simply saying that subjectivity is as important
to image collection structure as complete objectivity. We speak to that issue
in these final chapters.

CHAPTER ELEVEN

MASTER AND MASTERPIECE

*There is no way of determining in advance which detail is relevant to an
aesthetic interest; every detail can and ought to play a part.*
  Roger Scruton, "The Photographic Surrogate," *Salisbury Review*, 1987

ISTORICALLY, HUMANS HAVE treated seeing as a learning experience. In that regard, the knowing viewer is expected to pass that
knowledge to the unknowing viewer, and most of our institutions are founded on that premise. However, an image can never be known,
it can only be subjected to interpretation. And when boundaries are put
around interpretation, knowledge attributes that represent the aura of that
image are undermined.

We hope that our readers do not misconstrue our argument. We do not
advocate that viewers of an image (photo, painting, sculpture, craft, film, or
other viewable medium) should be told that a bus is a truck or a house is a
boat, even though both are quite plausible. What we are advocating is that
the seeing mind is never wrong (barring physiological impairment); yet, it is
sometimes confused.

Because vision relies on memory, and there is never a single approach
to something remembered, engagement with an image is necessarily constructed around personal, political, economic, dramatic, everyday, and/or his-
toric aspects that associate images to viewers. The literature, however,
mostly speaks to how those same aspects associate the image with its creator
and expects viewers to "buy in" to those interpretations as though the viewer's own interpretations have little merit or value. For example, museums
throughout the world are filled with images of so-called masterpieces around
which collections are structured. What makes a "masterpiece" worthy of
being the focal point of a collection? The answer resides in the definition of
masterpiece:

1. Historically, a piece of work presented to a medieval guild as evidence of qualification for the rank of master;
2. A work done with extraordinary skill.

What does not fit the definition of either masterpiece or master is a work
that represents a particular historical era, culture, creative style, change from

the accepted norm, point of view, or radical state of mind. Each of these conditions can offer insight into the reason that a work exists, but it is not a characteristic, feature, or attribute of the work (image) itself.

With that consideration in mind, we can easily organize groups of images in a collection into the periods during which they were created, the cultural influences that molded their creation, the styles or movements that set the works apart from others, or the materials from which the works were composed. Most traditional approaches to major institutional collections focus on these conditions associated with an image without addressing focal opportunities that other viewers may engage in during the viewing experience and that could be used to structure a body of works from similar points of viewer focus. Very seldom do we see a Japanese woodblock print, a contemporary photograph, and an Impressionist oil painting hanging in the same room as part of a homogeneous grouping of common visual elements. More likely we would encounter the Japanese woodblock print in the Asian or Far East part of the collection, the photograph in a section with other photographs, and the oil painting in a room or section with other Impressionist works. For example, the Art Institute of Chicago. *Viewing of Maple Trees*, by Utagawa Kunisada, is a Japanese woodblock from 1835 and is part of the Asian Collection; *The Seine at Vernonnet*, by Pierre Bonnard, is an oil on canvas from 1930 and is in the European Painting Collection; and *Mendocino River*, by Carleton Watkins, is an albumen silver print from the American West in the 1860s, and is part of the Photography Collection. In each instance the features, characteristics, and attributes of those images create, for a viewing public, a homogeneous grouping of trees, water, sky, and panorama that would qualify the images to be part of the same collection, not separate ones.

To further expand this concept of structuring collections around image conditions in lieu of the visual elements the images contain, we return once again to Leonardo da Vinci's *Mona Lisa*, in which we have an example of master and masterpiece. Like most major institutional holdings, descriptive materials about the *Mona Lisa* include interpretations of the work. Those interpretations, for the most part, contain conditions that surround the work but are not necessarily part of the viewing experience. For example, the materials state the following:

- Seated woman in Florentine dress
- Enigmatic expression
- An instance of Leonardo da Vinci's sfumato technique
- Painted around 1505

Notice that the only features, characteristics, and attributes of the image itself are that it is a painting of a woman wearing a dress. All else can be construed as interpretive conditions associated with the image, which viewers may or may not consider as part of the visual experience unless so described by someone else or through other descriptive materials. Furthermore, if it is a reproduction of the *Mona Lisa* that is being viewed, it may no longer be a painting. Even the fact that the figure is seated is up for visual interpretation, because we have no evidence of what position the figure's legs are in from viewing this image even though parts of a supposed chair are in the visual field.

In addition, images are often given an important status based on the genre to which they are attached, not for the visual elements they contain. While landscape, wildlife, still life, portrait, and religious (sacred) are commonly used genres for structuring collections, genre categories such as grotesque (strange, ugly, or bizarre), kitsch (pretentious or in bad taste), trompe l'oeil (tricks the eye through optical illusion), and vanitas (a reminder that death is certain) are just as valid for structuring a collection. Newer genres continue to emerge, such as maximalism (bright, sensual, visually rich), eroguru (the macabre intermingled with sexual overtones), and urban vinyl (vinyl action figures that have found their way into museum collections such as the Tokyo Museum of Art and the Boston Museum of Fine Arts).

The concepts of master and masterpiece have always been given lofty pedestals in cultural settings that reward craftsmanship through notoriety, monetary gain, or both. Even the private collector is often quick to show off the pieces in a collection that may be known for what they represent in value, not for the nature of the visual engagement that can be generated by a guest viewer. We hearken back to the 1940s, when French painter Jean DuBuffet was attributed with the term *art brut*. The concept was meant to imply that art (images) can be created by individuals who are totally removed from any base of classical art, style, or trend, and from any constraints that may be imposed through cultural conditioning. Traditionally, that description would include prisoners, patients in psychiatric institutions, and other socially maladjusted individuals. However, we could also apply the art brut concept to any image viewer who is considered a prisoner of the culturally accepted norms of visual engagement with an image object and, further, who is considered to be intellectually maladjusted if unable to conform to the modes of interpretation provided while in the presence of that image object. Our point being: We don't always know what we are seeing, but we always see what we know. When it comes to structuring a collection of images, tradition has generally pointed us toward a "knowing" point of view, not a "seeing" point of view, when it comes to organizing, categorizing, and structuring a collection. From our perspective, there are no masters and there are no masterpieces. There are only images that have a point of origin and can be subject to a variety of interpretations. Interpretations have become the bulwark of collection structure.

QUALITY AND COLLECTION STRUCTURE

The preceding commentary on master, masterpiece, image, and interpretation acts merely as a prelude to quality and its place in organizing and structuring an image collection. What is quality? At this juncture, you may facetiously point out that quality is a matter of interpretation. Granted; however, we prefer to take that idea one step further:

> Quality is a value judgment based on conformance to a standard.

In that sense, collections are structured around the conformance to certain rules, policies, and procedures that underpin the collection as a whole before it is organized and used to make decisions about what should be included and what should be excluded from the collection. While an individual may be an avid collector of celebrity portraits, he or she may balk at including a "Velvet Elvis" in that collection. The collection standards just won't allow it.

This whole issue of collection quality standards not only influences what will be acquired, displayed, stored, or sold; it also can have a direct impact on how the collection is organized and accessed. This somewhat convoluted path leads us to some significant questions we will pose shortly. First, let us stop and conduct a form of thought experiment. Suppose that you have been asked to put a collection together that will be on display in a new corporate headquarters building or a set of offices in a university or some similar setting of your own design. For this we will use the collection of forty-eight images made by professional photographers in the display below.

One of your first collection decisions will have little to do with the actual images available: will the images carry thematic or production value similarities or will they simply be a set of images interesting only in their own right? If thematic resonance from place to place is the goal, what is the theme? Is it easily articulated? Will there be numerous images that most viewers would recognize as exemplars of the theme? If the similarity is to be found in production values, can you articulate those? Will "bright and colorful" or "sober and ennobling" be sufficient, or will you require careful measurement of color values and textures? Once questions such as these have been considered, the images themselves can be addressed. We will assume that high quality is desirable, but we must ask just what that will mean. A few possible scenarios will seed thoughts on selection and quality.

The first image in our source group is a flower, a salmon pink iris. There are two other images of blossoms available, a Christmas cactus bloom and a daffodil poking through a chain link fence. On the face of it, these would seem to be a "natural" grouping. There are some points to consider though. The daffodil image is distinctive in having the manufactured object, the fence, so prominent. The daffodil and the iris are both outdoors, while the Christmas cactus is indoors. What if you wanted to work on colors

rather than on objects or themes? The iris and the Christmas cactus together are almost perfect color matches for the pink and red in the image of the wall with graffiti and the abandoned shopping cart. While the graffiti and shopping cart might not be objects that would be appropriate for any particular setting, the two blossom images do have color in common with the graffiti image. In fact, there is also a close match with the image of the old man and young man sitting at a diner counter; however, that image has a problem. It is out of focus, thus not likely to be considered of high enough production value. It was taken by a professional photographer as a "grab" shot;

there was a hope that the focus might work, and the desire to have a memory of the moment warranted taking a chance. The image still works as a memory piece but would not be a part of the photographer's portfolio.

Suppose the chosen theme is water. What images might we choose? There is an image of a woman walking on a cold and dreary beach. While it might engage one in thought or represent the natural elements, it is not a subject that would normally be associated with the office suite scenario; nor does the color palette present "bright and welcoming." The image of runners coming over a steeplechase hurdle presents colors that are bright and engaging, and the subject might even have some relationship to pressing on through adversity or delighting in ability. There is some water in the bottom portion of the image. There is an image of a man and a woman in a canoe on an autumn day on a beautiful lake; however, the image was made with a low-end snapshot camera and would not produce a sharp image of more than four inches by five inches—not likely an office suite size, though it might work for some settings. Next might be the high-resolution image of a flooded antique gas station. The colors are bright and there is a lot of water and the composition, particularly with the reflections, are well accomplished within artistic standards. Yet one would have to think about whether a flood scene is appropriate to the setting of the collection. What about the two images of single seagulls? These raise interesting issues. Neither shows any water, yet gulls are highly associated with water. Is that enough? Research that we have conducted, in which we asked participants to note terms that went with an image, shows that people will often use tags for associated objects or actions that are not actually in the image. Perhaps in the case of a water theme, the connection of gulls to water is sufficiently strong. The image with the larger gull is well within the norms for composition and resolution, while the flying gull image is problematic because of the cluttered background. What about the grayscale image of a canal beside some nineteenth-century mill buildings? The composition is classic for the period, the resolution is acceptable; but is a grayscale image appropriate for the design scheme and the image of the organization? What of the birch tree leaning out over a lake? Here we have nearly the whole frame filled with water, along with a tree at an odd angle that draws in the viewer's gaze. Is the odd angle of the tree just too much? What of the small white kayak on the edge of blue water? The resolution is fine and the white on blue is a clean, refreshing, and invigorating color palette? The possible companion image of the same white kayak together with a large blue boat has a more classically engaging composition, but close examination shows that it was made with a disposable cardboard camera for fear of damaging the high-end camera. Does the image of a kayak on a dock work? The lighting is open shade; is that too gloomy? Do the cars in the parking lot cause too much clutter? Would cropping the image to get rid of the cars work? What about the image of bird tracks that come to the water's edge? Is there enough water in the image? Is the disappearance of the tracks too ominous? These are but some of the questions that might come into play within the given scenario.

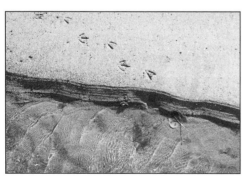

QUESTIONS FOR SELECTING THE CORPORATE COLLECTION

1. *Using quality as a guideline, which of the images above would you include in that new corporate collection?* Our thought exercise should make it evident that "quality" is a multifaceted concept. Notions of composition and suitability of subject are highly variable. Perhaps less variable are the physically measurable properties such as resolution, exposure, and color values, though even these may be viewed with greater or lesser latitude by different people.

2. *Using "created by a professional photographer" as the quality standard, now which images would you include in that corporate collection?* Again we are left without a clear, unambiguous response. Professional photographers, even those of some renown, may make images that are lacking in some physically measurable facet, that are well crafted but inappropriate in subject, or are "just not what we're looking for."

3. *Using "images that are interesting and unusual" as the quality standard, which images would you now include in that corporate collection?* Yet again, the issues are not given to binary solutions. What is interesting will depend as much on the viewer as it will on the subject of the photograph and its treatment. The surgery patient with the electromagnetic field generator might be quite interesting to some people, though not likely to surgeons and nurses; it would be too personal or medical for many office suite collections and far too mundane for a suite of offices in a medical facility. The image of a photographer and an inflated latex glove is unusual but has too little context for many viewers, though some are intrigued by "just what's going on?" The armadillo portrait might well be interesting and unusual for people on either coast or the northern portion of the United States, but would be of only passing interest to many residents of Texas. The pewter kayaker on a glass plate over the words "relative humidity" is unusual and perhaps of some interest, but is that enough, in and of itself, to warrant inclusion in a particular collection?

We hope that this little exercise has presented sufficient evidence that the viewing audience, while having the right to determine what constitutes a quality image, may not have the authority to implement their judgments. They are only given rights to view images that others have determined are worth seeing based on a set of standards that become the conditions for viewing and are not inherent parts of the image itself. Although quality may be in the eye of the beholder, it may be somewhat elusive for the beholder of a collection of images, depending on the standards used to construct it.

CHAPTER TWELVE

A WORD ABOUT THE NEEDY

A LTHOUGH MUCH HAS been said about how image collections can be structured, we have only made passing comments on the issues surrounding access to images that reside in collections. Image retrieval, especially from large database collections, has become a major topic in academic disciplines that require such access. The need to retrieve a particular image, sets of images, or an example of an image type is the most common query to an image database. Hence, the structure of an image database collection is important to the success of those queries. An entire business field, called digital asset management (DAM), has recently emerged as a result of these large and extensive database structures. The main concern for DAM professionals is the creation of efficient and effective ways to store, find, and share digital assets that include artwork, photos, logos, presentations, text documents, and even e-mails, and to keep such systems secure from unwanted outside intrusion. Without delving into the intricacies of such programs, it is important to note that these systems are, as has been the custom in the design of relational databases, dependent on "keywords" to identify the object needed.

In the traditional mode of document searching, *keywords* are defined as the significant words or phrases that appear in a title, abstract, subject heading, content notes, or document text in a bibliographic database. However, when building an image database to provide access to images in a collection, the keyword concept requires reinterpretation. Note that we are not saying words are a necessity or a superior form of representation; rather, we are only saying that they are used frequently.

MEMORY MARKERS

The human brain, in support of the human senses, mobility, and sustenance, functions primarily as a thinking machine. That machine, as it has developed over time, has served us mostly in support of listening, seeing, saying, and doing. Most human beings need to do all of those things, barring any unforeseen misfortunes or defects stemming from birth. In the context of needing, searching, and eventually retrieving images from a collection of images, we should consider each of these thinking machine functions.

When we hear something that we consider important, we have a tendency to remember it in part or in its entirety. When we see something to which we have paid attention, we tend to remember it in part or in its entirety. When we say something in a meaningful situation, we tend to remember it in part or in its entirety; and when we do something, we tend to ... you get the picture. In each case, our memories bring the past into the present in order to accomplish something in the future. How does all this relate to images and the structures of image collections?

How we consider the place of words in designing more effective image retrieval systems should reflect reinterpretations of how keyword searches are performed to access images from a large database collection of images. Such reinterpretations could begin with how we think and how we remember. The following diagram is only one possible example of how this concept can be illustrated and put to use in a functioning image retrieval system stemming from the concepts already discussed.

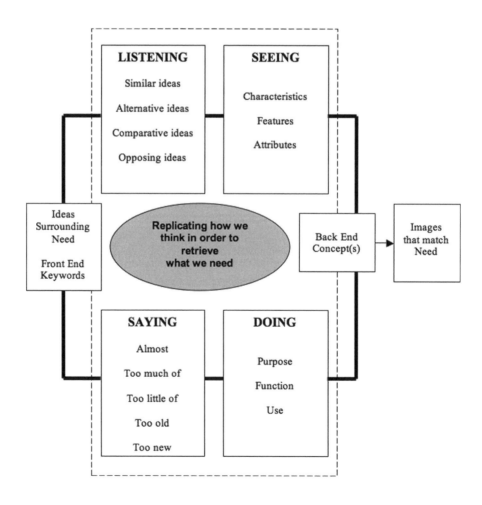

ECONOMY OF INFORMATION

One way to define *information economy* is the least number of words needed to define a concept. Another might be the least number of images needed to tell a story. In each case, the keyword that associates economy with information is *least*. If least is an obvious and recognized goal when it comes to information, then why have we experienced exponential growth in the number of publications and images that are available for public consumption?

We believe the answer lies in an expansion of the phrase resulting from its definitions. Most of us desire and look for an *economy of information needs*, the ability to express our wants and retrieve our desires in the most efficient and effective way. The result of this unique human characteristic is the establishment of niche markets of information in order to meet the direct informational needs of an individual. We no longer settle for just the text and images in a sports publication. Instead, we seek out, based on economy of information needs, only those publications that cater to the sports we enjoy viewing and reading about. Esoteric titles such as *Fly Tyer*, *Gun Dog*, *Northwest Runner*, and *Shark Diver* speak to the specific, sometimes very narrow, information needs of individual subscribers without the cognitive clutter that often accompanies more general titles devoted to the genre of interest.

This phenomenon is not exclusive to sports. It is pervasive in terms of everything we encounter on a day-to-day basis and for which we need information. The growth of and interest in online search engines is another prime example of how people attempt to attain economy of information needs. Those information needs can be the best price for an impending purchase, the best way to travel to a specific location, a quick way to select and send an appropriate gift to a friend, and, of course, the latest up-to-date information on just about any subject matter worldwide.

One difficulty we currently face, however, is that these needs currently cannot be fully satisfied with these same search engine concepts when it comes to needing a specific image to fulfill a specific need. Although many professionals have diligently pursued perfection in this arena, no one has created anything close to the ideal solution. We would suggest—not as search engine designers, but as image viewers and retrievers—that more attention be given to how people think about images and less to the ways of designing more effective programming algorithms for searching words.

POWERS OF SELECTION

In addition to the difficulties associated with finding the right image that meets a specific need in a large database of images, there is the issue of pure quantity when it comes to selection. Most of today's online image search engines are capable of producing voluminous results that may ultimately require tedious perusal on the part of a searcher in order to meet the specific need. The viewer may well make a quick cost-to-gain computation and seek another search method rather than examine hundreds of images. On the other hand, since visual pattern recognition is a significant attribute of human brains, some searchers may well decide that examination of a large retrieved set is more fruitful than starting over.

When it comes to building a database of images that is searchable, the location of images in the collection structure is not as important as it is when creating the physical collection. What is more important, however, is deciding how many access points will be provided for finding and retrieving the individual images in that database collection. For example, an online view of the Metropolitan Museum of Art, New York (www.metmuseum.org) provides a search utility that continually refines the search by providing a series of links to the collection based on the information needs of the searcher. Our first attempt was to look at "Portraits" in the collection, which took us to a page indicating 2,019 possibilities with a link to the "Permanent Collection" that accounted for 910 of those possibilities, a link to a "Timeline of Art History," with 670 possibilities, and a link to "Features," which held 439 possible solutions in relation to *portraits*. When we clicked on the "Permanent Collection" link, we were directed to a page that further refined the possibilities for satisfying our information needs, beginning with a link to 599 European Paintings that were assumed to be portraits. Although 599 results are still quite cumbersome, the Web page did provide additional search capabilities for refining that quantity by the name of the artist or by date.

Although we are not advocating the Metropolitan's search engine as the best possible solution for searching a collection, we are indicating that their methods for approaching such a best practice are worth noting. However, on a negative note, we also did a search using the word "heroism" and found no matches. We then used the word "heroic" and were greeted with thirteen results. Not to be deterred, we also entered "hero" and were directed to sixteen results. Our first comment is that we were surprised that there was no overlap between the thirteen image results and the sixteen image results. Second, we suspect that given the opportunity to browse the 2,456 items listed as part of European Art in the Permanent Collection we would be able to find, from our point of view, more than sixteen items that could be considered examples of hero, heroic, and/or heroism.

IMAGE FACTURE

Denis Diderot, the French philosopher and writer said, "*chaque peintre a sa facture, qui le distingue des autres artistes,*" which translates roughly into "each painter has a manner of painting characteristic to that painter and distinguishes him from other painters." We further propose that every image, whether painting or other medium, that meets the eye of a viewer has its own "facture," its own way of being distinguishable from other images. Philosophically, as well as physically, this distinction eliminates the sameness often associated with copies, duplicates, representations, prints, engravings, etchings, photos, numbered editions, giclees, and any other description that implies that two or more images of the same thing are the same. Each possesses its own unique provenancial characteristics that separate it from other likenesses. But, we might ask: Is that a good thing?

The importance of this distinction in relation to image collections is that collectors often remove like objects and images from the viewing public because they are considered duplicates. But, as evidenced in online image searching, the "same" image may appear often as part of the results of a keyword search. For example, Van Gogh's *The Starry Night* resides in the Museum of Modern Art, New York, but a Google search for the same image indicated 5,570 results, of which 400 were viewable. How many starry nights did Van Gogh paint? More importantly, why are we being inundated with "image facture" when we are only interested in seeing one image? Preferably the one that hangs in the Museum of Modern Art!

LEVELS OF IDENTIFICATION

With an ability to go more places and do more things than ever before, we are often faced with the ordeal of satisfactorily identifying ourselves for purposes of safety, protection, or accomplishment. We often forget that such identity images are the basis for structuring all sorts of collections. We have head shots in the entertainment industry, mug shots in the penal system, passports, driver's licenses, credit cards, high school and college yearbooks, and a

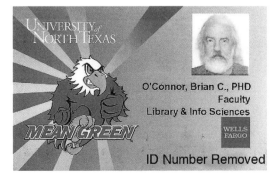

vast array of other fraternal organizations, accrediting agencies, or governmental entities that require that members or employees be "identified" by an image of themselves.

Of course, the photograph taken at any particular time may well not present a recognizable two-dimensional projection of the face at some other time. Here the picture from my high school days is a reasonable representation of my head and shoulders in 1965. If the store clerk who asked for my driver's license yesterday to verify the use of my credit card had compared my 2007 head and shoulders to this photograph, I would likely have left the store empty-handed. On the other hand, somebody looking through the yearbook collection in the archives of the Manchester Public Library would be very surprised if they were to come across my 2007 image in the 1965 yearbook.

These types of collections also need attention to their structure if access to the collection is a frequent requirement. Should images in the collection be arranged in alphabetical order by last name? Should a unique identifying number be attached to all individuals? Is there a concern for where and when people were born, a current address, a phone number, an e-mail address? Do characteristics such as height, weight, color of hair, and ethnicity need to be included? Do unique identifying marks need to be included?

We often forget that these identity images are part and parcel of the image collection landscape and that these collections tend to yield their own unique requirements, similar to the rules followed by a school of art. For

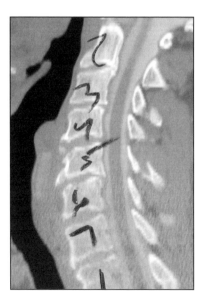

example, the passport photo is normally a specific size and shot from the shoulders up. The mug shot is usually composed of two or three images, including frontal view and one or two profile views, with height and identification number included. Yearbook images usually portray formal rather than casual dress.

Users often need to penetrate an identity database of images to access a specific individual or characteristic that defines a group of individuals. Attention paid to the structure of those collections at the design stage is an essential ingredient for making access to the right images successful at the time retrieval and use are eventually required.

These examples and numerous others (iris scans, traffic violations, satellite photos, x-rays, CAT scans, etc.) point to the continued and exponential growth of images that are available for capture, collection, and viewing.

The challenge will continue to be that of prompt access to an image or images that meet a specific need, which of necessity will engender more powerful hardware, more intelligent software, and more flexible collection structures.

PART V

LESSONS FROM THE FUTURE

Western culture is a culture of images, a culture firmly in the grip of photo-technologies for producing them.
Patrick Maynard, *The Engine of Visualization*, 1997

Given that recent advances in digital technology have provided a major impetus to the purchase and use of devices for capturing and storing images (cameras, video recorders, cell phones, handheld devices, and photo editing equipment), we present the following facts and posit the residuals:

1. In 2003 there were 50 million digital camera units sold worldwide (*Digital Photography Review*, 2004), up from 5 million units in 1999.
2. Mobile phones with built-in camera capabilities now number over 300 million. Over 80 percent of cell phones sold today include camera imaging of some sort, whether it is a stand-alone camera or one capable of video as well. It is projected that by 2009, there will be one billion camera cell phone units. (www.mobileimagingreport /Mobile_Imaging.htm).
3. No one knows the exact quantity of images on the Internet, but it numbers in the billions.
4. No one knows the number of digital images captured on a daily basis and saved in computerized files for later viewing and sharing with others.
5. No one knows the number of useful images that are captured, stored, and never looked at again, though some research suggests it is a large number.

6. The number of images identified in 5 will continue to grow exponentially until the methods used to organize, access, and retrieve those images are improved.

We are an image-based public. We remember with pictures of past events. We will not hesitate to rush into our homes under threat of fire or flood just to save our cherished images of people and times long gone. That era, however, is soon to depart. With digitized still images and video devices, we can now capture the full panorama of a single life, birth to death, and upload it to a Web-based archive. With cell phone cameras, security cameras, webcams, and wireless wearable cams, every event and experience can be subject to image capture. Nothing we can see with our eyes will go unnoticed. Hmm, where did those 8mm films of the kids go? Did they ever get converted to videotape? Did that videotape ever find its way onto a DVD? And what ever happened to the wedding photos, the birthday pictures, and the vacation memorabilia? Not to worry. Today you can throw those shoeboxes and photo storage containers away and just log on to the Internet and choose from Kodak Gallery, Snapfish, WinkFlash, DotPhoto, PhotoWorks, Shutterfly, Smugmug, WebPhotos, or Flickr, just to name a few that were up and running when this book was written. Upload your photos, put them in albums, and share them with family and friends—and the rest of the world!

Or not. Perhaps some aspects of the sharing of paper prints of photographs have not yet been accounted for. Perhaps the handwritten notes on the back speak volumes—"Yes, that is the same style mom always wrote in." Perhaps all the technological advancements in digital storage, retrieval, and manipulation still overlook representational capacities of paper photographs. This seems unlikely, yet we ought not to simply overthrow one modality for another without some thought to the consequences.

CHAPTER THIRTEEN

A MATHEMATICS OF IMAGE STRUCTURE

WITHOUT THE EXPERIENCE of viewing an image, any approach to defining its structure is severely limited. It may be felt, it may be smelled, and it may be tasted, but without the sensory input entailed in viewing an image, its structure lacks any robustness from a cognitive viewpoint. We can certainly structure an image collection based on feel, smell, and/or taste, but then galleries, museums, and the world of digitized images would collapse, and the impact on personal image collections would be devastating.

Hence, while most would consider viewing an image as an art, we could argue that it is, in fact, a science—a science that structures an image as a total viewing experience that begins with the sensory input associated with seeing, extends to the cognitive processes associated with interpreting what is being viewed, and finally becomes the verbal expression of what is being interpreted as a result of what is being seen. The underlying framework for this approach is based on the assumption that an act of understanding is mediated by the parts and pieces of an image. From that assumption, we posit that the structure of an image could be synthesized mathematically as follows:

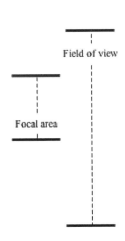

Field of view

Focal area

Image observation in total (O_t) is the sum of what is observed (sensory input) from focal attention (O_f) in association with the entire visual field (O_v):

$$O_t = O_f + O_v$$

The interpretation of what is observed (I_{Ot}) is composed of complementary, competing, and/or opposing points of cognition ($I_{p1} + I_{p2} + \dots I_{pn}$) resulting from what has been observed in total. These various points of cognition coincide with what others have called the basic elements, or native elements of visual sensory input such as shape, pattern, color, texture, size, luminance, distance, and clarity. Once the "seeing" has been performed, thinking is able to kick in, leading to an interpretation of what is being seen. This is not to imply, in any fashion, that the act of seeing and interpreting is a sequential operation, but for the purpose of discussion, it is important to note that one cannot interpret something until it is presented.

Interpretation of an observed image may be thought of as being composed of five distinct cognitive viewpoints, as follows:

Personal viewpoint

(P_v)—my unique interpretation as a summation of the following viewpoints, where $P_v = C_v + W_v$

Cultural view (C_v)—based on cultural/societal overtones
World view (W_v)—common to all regardless of culture and experience

Etymological viewpoint

(N_v)—rooted in the language and grammar of interpretation (what it is), that is, the naming of objects within an image

Experiential viewpoint

(K_v)—what is known by the viewer as opposed to what others may know in terms of knowledge and experience associated with the image being viewed

Emotional viewpoint

(E_v)—an autonomic response to the viewed image, producing an effect that may or may not affect interpretation, that is, fear, grief, love, sadness, and so forth

Locative viewpoint

(L_v)—an associative reaction to the viewed image (where and when), causing the viewer, sometimes consciously and sometimes subconsciously, to place the image in a specific location and time

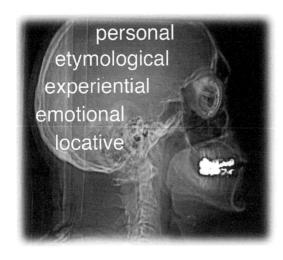

Image interpretation as it encompasses a total observation (I_{Ot}) =

$$P_v + N_v + L_v + E_v + K_v$$

These viewpoints combine in varying degrees to form a cognitive impression of the visual experience. Hence, visual experience (V_E) equals observation in total (O_t) plus the interpretation of that observation (I_{Ot}).

$$V_E = O_t + I_{Ot}$$

For many visual experiences, the process ends with interpretation. However, considering that this is a discussion of images and image collections that may exist in the public domain, the mathematics of image structure must also include an equation of expression that extends beyond mere mutual interpretation. Using the familiar phrase "a picture is worth a thousand words," the total visual experience should include the ability to express (verbally) what has been seen, as shown in the illustration below.

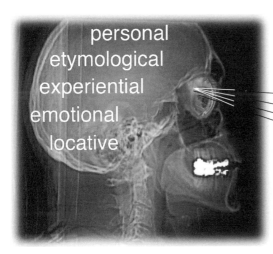

With shifts of focal area and some processing through views, I could say:

"That's my mother, brother, and me at Christmas many years ago in New Hampshire. Nice."

By using the notations above, the words used to express (W_x) the visual experience can then be added as follows:

$$V_E = O_t + I_{Ot} + W_x$$

While we might posit that the additive nature of these cognitively processed elements are associative and/or commutative, the literature abounds with findings that point to a more parallel processing of visual data, a type that is nonlinear and could be influenced from time to time by which aspect of interpretation is garnering the greater cognitive attention in combination with the visual focus. Having said that, we will conclude our comments on the mathematical nature of image structure in order to direct more attention to image collection structure.

Why have we taken this approach to image structure? The answer is semantically complex but visually simple. Images are not words. Considering that issues surrounding image collection structure entail concepts that include image storage, image retrieval, archiving, cataloguing, indexing, classifying, and the development of subject headings, thesauri, and taxonomies, we find that words, in some form or fashion, require merging with images. Without the above approach, it is a daunting task to match words with images that extend beyond descriptive references to the objects in the image and the history associated with its creation, collection, and physical properties with regard to film, photographs, paintings, sculpture, and other image collectibles. This is because words are not inherent in pictures; they are not native elements of photographs. To do a reasonable job of representing a word document we need only extract the words, count them, toss out everything but the nouns, and use the most frequently occurring nouns as descriptors. Since words are not inherent in pictures, we cannot simply extract them from the pictures.

We believe the value added by presenting this mathematical approach to image structure is the laying of a foundation from which to build an image collection and ways to structure how such collections can be accessed by viewers and patrons. We also point out that the notations included in this approach, while not homologous, are analogous to other attempts to resolve the dilemma of using words to define images.

CHAPTER FOURTEEN

IMAGE EXCESS AND COLLECTION ACCESS

In everything the middle course is the best; everything in excess brings trouble.

Titus Maccius Plautus, Roman comic poet (254–184 BCE)

I F YOU TOOK the time and effort to peruse the preceding chapters, you noticed that our approach to structures of image collections focused on the language elements that have traditionally been used to create and maintain those collections. We have also gone to great lengths in short paragraphs to emphasis how "meaning" in association with an image has different connotations in contrast with how meaning is construed in relation to textual materials. In essence, a word is a word, whereas an image can be described by a multitude of words. As technological advances provide the viewing public with more and more opportunities to access collections of images, more and more interpretations of those images are not only possible, but might well be a mandate for the development of more robust storage and retrieval systems.

Although inroads have been made by ignoring the words associated with images and looking at low-level image features such as color, shape, and texture, these approaches still remain on the trailing edge of what most

system users require when searching an image database. It is important to note after the prior chapters that the structure of an image collection, whether physical or digital, is still the product of an organizational process that stems from human cognitive processes, that is, we often think in words, so we are most likely to organize and search using words. Techniques such as content-based image retrieval (CBIR), also known as query by image content (QBIC) and content-based visual information retrieval (CBVIR), have provided limited solutions in specific settings. But for the most part the digital community is still struggling with uncovering the most efficient and effective metadata (word) solutions for storing and accessing image objects in a computerized or Internet-based environment.

One of the immediate, but not obvious, challenges today is access to items in diverse image database collections that contain similar objects but may not be accessible without knowledge that is additional to the image itself. In the public sector, for example, there are paintings by Jan Weenix (1642–1719) in the collections at the Lichtenstein Museum, the Ackland Art Museum at the University of North Carolina, and the Philadelphia Museum of Art. Each of these Weenix paintings can be found in rooms designated variously at each of the above museums as The Painting Gallery in the Academy of Fine Arts, European and American Painting, Johnson Collection, and Gallery 267. In one case, that structure is based on the period of time in which the work was created. In another case, the structure of the collection is based on the name of the family who owned the art objects. Yet, the other collections in this example were structured around the geographic location in which the artist resided or the genre of the art object. If, however, an individual image seeker was interested in a viewing experience that included hunting trophies, he or she would have a difficult time accessing these individual paintings or the large representative body of Weenix paintings that are part of the Wallace Collection, London.

Similar issues can be seen currently in the private sector when image collections are uploaded to Internet-based photo sites such as Flickr. The home page asks: "Find a photo of____" and you are prompted to enter a keyword or phrase. For example, upon entering the words "black cat," you will be given access to over 35,000 photos in the Flickr database that have been designated as "black" and "cat"; however, you may or may not have access to additional publicly available images of Jack, Cocoa, Max, Gatto, Anger, Chicken, Ci-Ci, Kat, gato, Ninja, kitty, Othello, Katz, Sitka, and a host of others.

Until other means and methods for structuring image collections are devised, language access to image excess will continue to plague or serve those in need of just the right image to fulfill their needs, pique their curiosity, or spark their creativity. In an attempt to put forward a utilitarian approach to what we consider an overwhelming need, we suggest the following new ways to look at old structures of image collections.

Viewing Communities

If we return to the preface of this book as a retrospective rather than an introduction, we can conclude our commentary by invoking once again our interpretation of Caesar's *Veni, Vidi, Vici* ("I arrived on the scene, I understood the situation, I was successful"). But we now enter a new age of digitization in which we can arrive on a Web page, be exposed to a database filled with images, and have no idea how to find what we are looking for, let alone understand what we are seeing. Or we can venture into a gallery or museum and see what someone has chosen for us to see but remain sequestered from the wealth of visual excitement that remains tucked away in a storeroom.

after the flood of 07

click here to add a description

© This photo is **public**. Change?
Uploaded on Apr 29, 2007 | Delete
8 views / 0 comments

Pilot Point

we were plagued by white pick ups all afternoon trying to do Better Light scans

© This photo is **public**. Change?
Uploaded on Apr 29, 2007 | Delete
7 views / 0 comments

Luckenbach
13 photos | Edit

Medium Cool Drive By
8 photos | Edit

Wild about Texas

click here to add a description

© This photo is **public**. Change?
Uploaded on Apr 29, 2007 | Delete
8 views / 0 comments

meat processing horse

click here to add a description

© This photo is **public**. Change?
Uploaded on Apr 29, 2007 | Delete
5 views / 0 comments

Wildcat Canyon
9 photos | Edit

Image collection structure is as much a function of what is viewable as it is a function of what is hidden from view. Each instance causes us to take a closer look at the viewing community that chooses or is allowed to associate itself with an image collection. There are several types of viewing communities that can lead to more efficient and effective ways to structure image collections

THE "I SEE IT AND I DON'T NEED TO UNDERSTAND IT" COMMUNITY

This community of viewers is very common and can be seen walking the streets every day. These viewers also compose populations of museum and gallery patrons wherein their specific interest lies in the viewing experience. These viewers need no signs, no descriptions, no tags, no label—in essence, no words of description to reap enjoyment (or disdain) for the images being viewed.

Structuring collections for this type of viewing community is all about *seeing* and less about organizing. This community wants to engage the images in the collection in a way that is visually pleasing and that allows full disclosure of the image elements without diversion and interference. Thus, image placement is more important than image organization and description to these viewers. The key cognitive element for these viewers is attraction or avoidance.

THE "I SEE IT AND I'D LIKE TO KNOW MORE ABOUT IT" COMMUNITY

This community of viewers is also very common and composes a large portion of what is gratuitously referred to as the "viewing public." Most public collections are structured around this type of viewing community. These viewers need their maps. They want to know where things are, what those things belong to, why they are there, and what they're all about.

Structuring collections for this community of viewers is all about *knowing*. Knowing the artist, knowing the image (title), knowing why it was created, and knowing that they have seen something worthwhile. The experience for this type of viewer must be both visual and cognitively enlightening for full pleasure to be gained from the engagement.

THE "I SEE IT AND I'D LIKE TO SEE MORE LIKE IT" COMMUNITY

This is an interesting viewing community because it is composed of viewers from both of the preceding populations. Those that are into only *seeing* may also want to see more examples of what they deem visually pleasing. And those who are into both seeing and knowing may also want to see more examples of what they just learned. It is for this latter audience that most public institutions that display works of art have been designed, with their collected works divided into knowledge groupings more than into visual groupings. Hence, we find galleries devoted to particular chronologies, specific art movements, individual countries, single artists, or single collectors, so that both seeing and knowing can be better organized from the institution's point of view.

However, the group of patrons that prefers seeing more of what they like (visually) is left to wander about in search of similarly pleasing experiences. Hence, they are penalized for seeing without knowing. We seldom, if ever, encounter a hall of mountain scenes, a gallery of waterfalls, or a bearded portrait room. This, of course, should not be construed as a call for such venues; but it should be considered as yet another way to structure image collections to suit a type of viewing community.

THE "I SEE IT, I'D LIKE TO KNOW ABOUT IT, AND THEN I'D LIKE TO SEE OTHERS RELATED TO THAT KNOWLEDGE" COMMUNITY

This last community of viewers may be considered by some to be the most intellectual of viewing audiences. They not only see the image objects and gather knowledge about them, but they also seek to expand that knowledge and their visual experiences by viewing other works that may or may not be the same but have a relationship to the original viewing. For these patrons of the arts or simply viewers of a collection of images, the inherent challenges of collection structure are self-evident. What are the connections to other works? What are the appropriate access points to those other works? And are all of those connections and access points useful to viewers within this community?

In this instance, it's all about seeing, knowing, understanding, and synthesizing a next step for accessing more. Once again, if there are billions of images available for viewing and millions of databases within which they reside, plus thousands of institutions that can be visited and hundreds of people that could supply direction, instruction, and information, then how, when, and where should collection structure begin?

CHAPTER FIFTEEN

WHAT'S THE USE?

WE HAVE EXPLORED, contemplated, asserted, and wondered much about collections of images. There is likely much that has been left unsaid. There is likely to be much that will develop shortly after we write our last words. *Geotagging*, which enables arranging and searching by global positioning coordinates, is blossoming. Photographs of social network friends will soon pop up on cell phones if the friends are within a specified physical distance, resulting in an intriguing collision between virtual and physical lives. Searching Web-based collections by camera model is already offering prospective buyers a new means of evaluation—if more people use camera X than camera Y to take the sorts of pictures I intend to take, camera X is likely a better choice for me.

With cameras in more and more devices, the very types of images may well change; more and more images may well be taken with no thought toward collection or retrieval. For example, I happened to be typing in a neurosurgeon's office that has a model of the area of my neck on which I had surgery, so I took a photo with the camera in my laptop just to send to a friend. Perhaps the image will survive cleaning up my files, perhaps not. This transient or ephemeral nature of many images made with cell phones, laptops, and other unobtrusive cameras means they may never be in collections other than in acqui-

sition order on the storage medium. Even that collection may well be deleted to make room for other ephemera. Collections may become virtual, in the sense of "Here is another picture of me now, just to show you where I am or what I see."

The quantitative change in ease of image use has begun to yield new forms of collection; so too has the quantitative change in access to digital images. I recently posted a picture to my Flickr

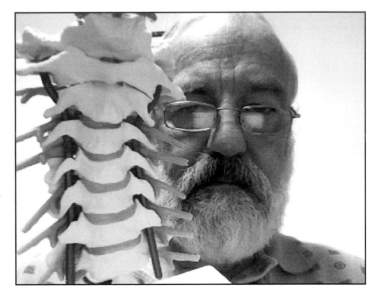

account; a colleague asked if he could post the link on his blog; hundreds of people I have never met had viewed the picture that same day. Several of those who viewed that image asked to become Flickr contacts on my account. In a strong sense, the one photograph has generated a collection of viewers, whose own images are now linked to some nonzero degree to my images, forming a metacollection.

A JOURNEY OF LOOKING

So we have journeyed from a collection of images whose medium allowed them to endure for millennia (though bear scratches and over painting did render them somewhat less than permanent) to images in media that can be made with trivial effort in highly manipulable media. The earlier collection was fixed in place, viewable only by those who could come to that place; the later collections are available to almost anyone in the world. The purpose of the earlier image collection is unknowable; the purposes of modern collections are myriad, some knowable and stated, others private.

We have considered several facets of collections, the images within collections, and those who make use of collections of images. Perhaps noticeable by their absence are rules or suggestions for construction of collections of images or the use of such collections. We have assumed structure to be a useful assemblage of parts; not only the physically tangible parts, the images, but also those who view, arrange, manipulate, transform, learn from, weep over, laugh at, and engage with the pictures. Collections of images do not simply appear; some person or group must assemble them. Images in a collection might be seen by a few people then by nobody for millennia and then be repurposed for use in a book. Images by a noted photographer or pictures of some notable event might be carefully gathered and displayed in a gallery or museum, while others may be sent from a cell phone or camera to the online version of a news network with essentially no curating other than linking the images to tags for object, place, and date. A viewer might stand in line for an hour to see a Diane Arbus or Ansel Adams show or to glance for a moment at the baby picture in an e-mail from a former student.

Suppose while you were walking you came upon a single photograph. Would you know the collection from which it came? There is a high probability you would not know. Of the billions of photographs made each year, only a very few achieve widespread recognition as pieces of art or journalism. Would you be able to think of a collection to which you might add the photograph? It is quite likely that you could, even if that were to be the collection of things you did not find interesting. Is it likely that you could think of one or more uses that you or a friend might be able to make of the photograph? Again, it is quite likely that the answer would be yes.

ONE LAST LOOK

We have provided several viewpoints describing how people tend to look at, collect, and organize images that depict a variety of styles, formats, genres, and media. One final note, however, is to remind readers that, regardless of the visual experience, there is a cognitive tendency to add those experiences to some type of memory collective that allows not "recollection" but "re-collection" at some later date. A "re-membered" visual experience may be summoned by words, by smell, by sound, or by touch; yet it would be virtu-ally impossible to identify those individualized mental image collections by their associated stimuli.

Additionally, it should be apparent after this reading that a single image object can render a multitude of mental re-collections and associated de-scriptive terms, all of which or none of which might suit the needs of an individual viewer.

Our concluding thought is that no matter what an image may be called, its ultimate placement in a structured collection resides in the answer to only one question:

What's the use?

We do not mean this as an expression of despair! Rather, we assert that this is the central question, the consideration from which all other facets of structure flow. Humans do things. Images help them do those things.

Panel of the Hand Stencil, Grotte Chauvet-Pont-d'Arc, slide no. 4.

INDEX

About the Authors

HOWARD F. GREISDORF is Director of Training at UniFocus in Carrollton, Texas.

BRIAN C. O'CONNOR is a Professor at the School of Library and Information Sciences, University of North Texas in Denton, Texas.